MY ANCESTORS WERE MANORIAL TENANTS

by Peter B Park

SOCIETY OF GENEALOGISTS ENTERPRISES LTD

Published by
Society of Genealogists Enterprises Limited
14 Charterhouse Buildings
Goswell Road
London EC1M 7BA

ISBN 1 903462 59 2

British Library Cataloguing in Publication Data
A CIP Catalogue record for this book is available from the British Library

About the Author

Peter Park has been involved in family history research for 30 years. He is a professional archive researcher and a Fellow of the Society of Genealogists. An experienced speaker on family history and associated topics. He is a past member of the Society's Executive Committee and former Chairman of its Publications and Lectures Committee.

Society of Genealogists Enterprises Limited is a wholly owned subsidiary of Society of Genealogists, a registered charity, no 233701

The cover illustration is from the court book of the manor of Torver in Lancashire. Lancashire Record Office, ref: DDHj, Torver court book 1740-53.

CONTENTS

PLATES

FIGURES

ACKNOWLEDGEMENTS

Few books such as this are written in isolation - and this is no exception. I have drawn on a range of primary and secondary sources, in particular the records of the manor of Torver in Lancashire and the books by I H Baker *(An introduction to legal history),* Eric Kerridge *(Agrarian problems of the sixteenth century and after),* A W B Simpson *(A history of the land law)* and Sidney and Beatrice Webb *(The manor and the borough)*

My thanks go to the staff of the Public Record Office and the County Record Offices of Cumbria (Barrow and Kendal), Gloucestershire, Lancashire and Surrey for their courteous help. The staff of the Walton on Thames branch of the Surrey County Library have willingly processed my requests for obscure books and papers. In cases such as this it is invidious to single out individuals, but I must pay special thanks to the staff of the Cumbria Record Office at Barrow who have cheerfully photocopied hundreds of pages of manorial records for me over the years.

I would like to thank the following individuals and organizations who have allowed me to use transcripts or facsimiles of their documents as illustrations: Brigadier C E Tryon-Wilson for Plate I (Beetham manor court book) and the Crown Estate for the cover illustration and Plates II-XII. Mr I S Yorke has kindly given me leave to use the Keevil and Bulkington material (Figure 1). The two lists of tenants used in Figure 3 are taken from Crown Copyright material and are used with the permission of the Controller of Her Majesty's Stationery Office. The Appendix, Figure 2 and the other extracts from the notebook of Earl Spencer's Steward are quoted by courtesy of the Surrey Record Office.

Since the first edition of this book, I have spoken at many family history society meetings about manorial records. In the question sessions after the talks many points have been raised regarding aspects of the records. I have taken the opportunity to include, or clarify, them in this second edition. My thanks to all those family historians who have made me aware of what they need to know, long may you keep asking questions.

Roy Hudlestone, Alan Reed and Chris Watts read an early draft of the text and Stella Colwell made suggestions for this second edition. Their constructive criticisms, suggestions and corrections were invaluable. Any mistakes in fact, spelling or grammar are entirely due to my failure to respond to their collective wisdom – I am truly indebted to them all.

ACKNOWLEDGEMENTS

INTRODUCTION

The manor was an institution that affected almost every aspect of the lives of our English ancestors. It determined their rents and who inherited their land, decided where they grazed their cattle and when they cut the bracken, checked the condition of their dwellings and waterways, mediated in their financial, slanderous or pugilistic disputes, dictated where their corn should be ground, defended them against a greedy landlord – and against one another, punished them with amercements or set them in the stocks and controlled the quality of their ale and bread. In an earlier age it also determined the occupations their sons should follow and whom their daughters might marry.

And yet, despite all this, manorial records are sadly under-used by family historians, the majority of whom do not utilise them. The reasons given usually include: 'my ancestors didn't own any land, they were only agricultural labourers'; 'the records are all in Latin – we didn't do it at my school'; 'there don't seem to be any for the parish in which I am interested'; 'I have only got back to 1806 and am still working on the parish registers, so I don't need them yet'.

These are misconceptions: there is normally very little personal information about the lord of the manor in the records, only an occasional description of his property, but there can be an enormous amount of detail about his tenants and others who lived on his land; the records are not just medieval documents, indeed in a number of manors they are as recent as 1926; Latin ceased to be used in 1734 and there are many documents in English before this date.

Many genealogical text books are almost off-hand in their treatment of manorial records, with phrases along the lines of 'when parish registers end, more experienced researchers may be able to get back to the thirteenth century by using the manor records'. As a result, the records have a reputation for being 'difficult' or 'advanced'. Many family historians who have used them admit that they did so, almost in desperation, after parish records had become less reliable, some time before 1700. This is a time when many manorial records *are* in Latin and often in an unfamiliar hand. They *are* 'technical' records and do require some expertise to get the best out of them, but by starting to use them earlier – in researching eighteenth, nineteenth, and even twentieth century ancestors – many problems associated with them can be minimised. The glossary provides definitions of many of the obscure terms encountered.

This booklet seeks to show that the effort spent finding out about this class of document can be well rewarded. Manorial records are especially useful in amplifying other records (they can often help to distinguish between people of the same name who appear in the pages of the parish registers with no identifiers) and may be the prime source when the registers are unreliable or missing. More than this however, they often enable us to put the everyday life of our ancestors under the microscope.

Needless to say, the records should not be used in isolation, but in conjunction with, for instance, parish registers, wills, quarter sessions papers etc. and a little common sense. A few words of warning are not out of place here – it is extremely unlikely that 'your' manor will have all the records described here – different customs and methods of record keeping as well as the ravages of time will have seen to that.

HISTORY

Most family historians are interested in the period beginning about 1540 and it is with the period since then that this book is primarily concerned. However, before discussing the records some earlier background history is essential for a better understanding of them.

Throughout the Middle Ages the almost universal territorial unit outside the incorporated towns in England and Wales was the manor; in Wales the manorial system was largely confined to those areas colonised by the Normans, mainly in Monmouthshire, the Vale of Glamorgan, the Gower and parts of the Cardigan coast.[1] The manor had its roots in the Anglo-Saxon period and vestiges of it still remain with us today. It was a feudal estate, normally agricultural or pastoral, held by a landlord – hence 'lord of the manor' – from the Crown either directly or via an intermediary. The estate might range in size from a few acres to over 100 square miles and could have only a handful of tenants or, as in the case of the manor of Wakefield in the West Riding of Yorkshire, as many as 1,400. The nature of the manor varied throughout the country according to the pattern of local agriculture and traditions of land tenure.

It is uncertain how many manors there were in England and Wales – estimates range from 25,000 to 65,000.[2] There were only about 12,000 parishes so there may have been be several manors in a particular parish. Conversely there might be a number of parishes, or parts of parishes, in a single manor. Family historians, used to dealing with 'the parish', often find difficulty in equating manor and parish. The manor is by far the older institution, with the parish growing out of one or a group of manors with the same lord (a lordship or a barony).

Developments during the Norman and medieval periods saw the term 'manor' come to mean a piece of landed property with tenants, over whom the landlord exercised jurisdiction through a manor court. These courts were of long standing (they had been in existence since Anglo-Saxon times), but, in time, they came to define the institution of the manor itself – without a manor court there was no manor.

The power to create new manors was lost by the end of the thirteenth century, although division or consolidation of existing ones did take place later.[3] During the sixteenth and early seventeenth centuries many old manors disappeared, especially in the Midlands Plain and other areas prone to enclosure.[4]

Most manors were divided into two parts, tenements which were small parcels of land worked by tenants, and the demesne which was reserved for the use of the lord. A manor was usually managed by the lord's steward who was normally a lawyer and it was he who sat in judgement in the manor court. On a large estate, with manors scattered around the country, the local management was in the hands of bailiffs. They were responsible to the steward for collecting the rents and the running of the demesne lands. They also represented the lord in day-to-day dealings with his tenants.

THE FEUDAL SYSTEM

In the narrowest sense, and the one that is relevant here, feudalism was a system of land tenure in which land was held in fief by vassals from lords. In the Middle Ages it was common across Europe and England was no exception. Feudalism was introduced to England by the Normans, but as early as 700, some forms of Saxon land tenure were based on obligations to perform services, and leasehold tenures limited to three generations were introduced by ecclesiastical landowners before 990.[5]

In England all land was owned by the King who enfeoffed the barons and other powerful men (they were the King's vassals). The manors under a baron's control were known as a barony. In their turn the barons enfeoffed lesser men, and thus became lords in their own right. Depending on the size of their holdings, the barons' vassals may in turn have enfeoffed others, becoming lords in their own turn. A subgroup of manors from a barony was a lordship. Thus the land-holding system was a pyramid, with the King at the apex, the barons and other great mesne (intermediate) lords in the middle while the base was formed of the poorer men – the lesser freemen, villeins and serfs.

The relationship between lord and vassal was complex. The lord had a duty to provide the holding, to protect the vassal and to do him justice in his court. In return he had the right to expect the services attached to the holding (usually military or agricultural) and to the various feudal incidents (incomes) such as the payment of a relief on transfer of the fief. In addition to services, the vassal owed homage to the lord and was required to pay suit to (attend) the manor court. By Tudor times the services on most manors had been commuted to cash payments or quit rents fixed by custom, and fiefs had become hereditary and could not be withheld from an heir who was willing to do homage:

> When the tenante shall make homage to his lord, he shal descende, and his hedde uncoveryd, and his lord shall sitte; and the tenante shall kneele before hym on both his knees, and holde his hands joyneteley togethere bytwene the handes of his lorde and shall say thus: Here you this my lorde: that I unto you shalbe faithfull and true: And shall bere you faith of the lande & ten't that I clayme to hold of you. And trulye shall do unto you the duties customes and s'vices due for the same at termes assigned, a help me godd and all saynts. And this done llett hym kysse the boke.[6]

Although the feudal system was abolished in 1660, these feudal ceremonies survived as long as the manor itself, for a lord might have cause to distrain if they were omitted. Thus as late as the nineteenth century:

> You shall swear to become a new Tenant to the Lord of this manor for the Est'e to which you are now admitted, you shall truly pay bear and do all such rents duties services heretofore due and of right accustomed and you shall in all things demean yourself as a faithful Tenant. So help you God.[7]

The lord had no right to eject a customary tenant who performed his services (paid his dues and swore his fealty etc.). Indeed, a lord who did so could be served with an action for trespass.[8]

After he had paid homage to his lord the tenant would swear an oath of fealty. Strictly speaking, fealty was an oath of allegiance to the Crown required from every tenant under the feudal system. When only fealty was given no services to the lord were involved, but care must be taken since homage was often referred to as 'fealty', particularly after the middle of the sixteenth century, as shown in Figure 1.[9]

Although the feudal system was in decline by the start of the period discussed here and was abolished by statute in 1660, its long use ensured that it continued to affect the content of manorial records until 1925.

Manor of Keevil	*to wit at the Court Leet & View of*
and Bulkington	*Frank Pledge of our Sovereign Lord the*
	King with the Court Baron of Wm Beach
	Esqr Lord of the said Manor there held the
24 Oct	*24th day of October in the 27th year of the*
	Reign of our Sovereign Lord George ye 3d by
1787	*the Grace of God of Great Britain France*
	& Ireland King Defender of the Faith
	And in the Year of our Lord 1787 before
	Francis Bayly Gent' Steward there
	To this court came Charles Blake and took
	of the Lord of the sd Manor by the delivery of his
formerly	*said Steward by the Rod according to the Custom of the*
Clifts	*said Manor All that one Messuage or Tenement*
	with the Garden and Orchard adjoining containing
	half an Acre (more or less) with the Appurtenances
	formerly in the Possession of William Dalmer
	afterwards of William Clift since of Catherine
	Clift his Widow afterwards of Ann Clift and
	late of Elizabeth Clift Daughters of the said William
	Clift To have and to hold the said Messuage or
	Tenement Garden Orchard and Premises with
	the Appurtenances unto the said Charles Blake
	aged about forty two Years Samuel Blake aged
	about ten Years and William Blake aged about
	five Years (Sons of the said Charles Blake) for and
	during the Term of their natural lives and the
	life of the longest Liver of them successively at the
	Will of the Lord according to the Custom of the
Rent 4s	*said Manor Yielding therefore yearly the Rent*
	4s And also yielding doing and performing also
	other Burthen Works Customs Suits and Services
	there foremerly due and of Right accustomed
	And for such Estate and Entry so to be had
	the said Charles Blake gave to the Lord for fine ten
fine	*pounds and ten shillings and so the said Charles*
£10 10s	*Blake was admitted Tenant thereof and did his fealty*
	to the Lord. But the fealty of the said Samuel
	& William Blake respectively is respited

***Figure 1**. Transcript from the manor court book of the manor of Keevil and Bulkington, Wiltshire, 24 October 1787.*

THE MANOR COURTS

Feudal law was largely established by local custom, with justice dispensed in local courts, two of which were the court baron and the court customary.[10] In practice these two courts were combined and referred to as the court baron. Technically the court baron had jurisdiction over the freemen while the servile tenants were subject to the court customary.[10] This combined court had two roles. It was concerned with the running of the manor as an estate (for instance, control of tenure, estate management, the appointment of manorial officials, etc.). It was here that the lord could enforce his rights to rents and services, although his tenants were protected by the customs of the manor. It also played a local, judicial role, hearing cases under customary law, although this seems to have fallen into disuse by the end of the seventeenth century. The court baron had the power to enact bye-laws for the regulation, administration and management of the manor. All tenants were obliged to attend, or give suit to, the combined court. The orders of the court were enforced by annually appointed officials, sometimes called barleymen or bylawmen.

From Saxon times the county hundreds had been divided into small groups of men, called tithings who were jointly responsible for the behaviour of individual members. The tithingmen or headboroughs (the head men from each tithing) attended a hundred court for a view of frankpledge twice a year to report on the state of law and order in their area. In large hundreds the view of frankpledge and a number of other activities, together known as the leet function, were often delegated to local manors.

It was from this delegation of jurisdiction that another local court, the court leet developed. It was the lowest level of Crown court dispensing criminal justice. It was here that petty common law offences such as assault, bloodshed, false weights and measures, gossip, eavesdropping and fouling the waterways were tried. The penalty for such offences was the pillory, stocks or a small amercement. More serious crimes were referred to the quarter sessions or the assizes. The court could also settle disputes between tenants involving sums of money of less than forty shillings. In theory, since this was a Crown court, the lord could be brought before the court leet of his own manor – he could not appear before the court baron which was his own property.

Every male over the age of sixteen, who had lived on the manor for a year and a day – not just the tenants – was obliged to attend the court leet. By Magna Carta the court should have been held every six months, but in practice may have been held only once a year. It appointed law and order officials, in particular the constable or headborough, who were responsible to the justices.

The authority from which each court derived its power is shown quite explicitly at the top of Figure 1: 'The Court Leet and View of Frankpledge of our Sovereign Lord the King with the Court Baron of Wm Beach Esqr Lord of the said Manor.' In both courts the amercements that were levied provided an income for the lord.

Courts originally met in the open, but once written records were kept it became necessary to hold them indoors. They were sometimes held in the manor house, but the local inn, school or church was often pressed into service. The court was sometimes ceremonially opened at an ancient place and then adjourned indoors. In many cases a special courthouse was used, such as that built by the monks of Furness Abbey at Hawkshead in Lancashire or the Moot Hall at Wakefield.

The court baron and court leet often sat in a combined session and the records of their proceedings were sewn in the same rolls or bound in books. In later years, as their power waned, the two were often merged into one undifferentiated court – Figure 1. However, it is important to remember that they were distinct courts and that not all manors had a court leet which was technically a Crown court, delegated for convenience.

The Tudor period saw the expansion of central government and reorganisation of local administration. Duties were assigned to the justices in each county and to the appointed officials of each parish or township. The result was that the manor courts lost much of their earlier responsibilities. In particular, the functions of the courts leet were taken over by the quarter and petty sessions with the constable being appointed by the parish vestry. Common and statutory law made inroads into customary law, so that the judicial role of the courts baron became obsolete, leaving them responsible solely for the administration of the estate. The enclosures of the eighteenth and nineteenth centuries deprived thousands of courts baron of their business connected with agriculture and the transfer of copyhold tenancies. The manorial courts were finally abolished in 1977 by the Administration of Justice Act.

This did not happen overnight. The courts baron retained importance as the only means for the conveyance of copyhold land until 1925. Many courts leet heard cases well into the eighteenth century and some into the nineteenth; it was as late as 1842 before an Act of Parliament took the right of appointment away from the surviving courts; the court leet of Ulverston in Lancashire was appointing constables for a number of townships until at least 1837.[11] In many districts there was obviously administrative interaction between the manor court and the parish vestry for many years.

LAND TENURE

We have seen that the manor was landed property with tenants and it is as tenants, rather than as lords, that most of our ancestors will have had dealings with it. Land tenure is a very complex subject. For those interested in its legal aspects, the books by Baker, Kerridge and Simpson, listed in the bibliography, are very helpful.

Under the feudal system all land was owned by the Crown – all other persons were tenants with rights protected by the law. Land tenure, that is the manners and conditions of service by which lands were held of their lords, were extremely varied. Tenure was either frank (free) or base and held at the will of the lord according to the custom of the manor.

The majority of tenures were base and referred to as customary. Most, but not all, customary tenants in the early modern period had copies of the entry in the manor court records regarding their holdings – they were thus called copyholders. For most family history purposes the terms can be regarded as interchangeable; one of the few times the subtle distinction might cause family historians a problem would be a dispute over a tenancy in the Court of Chancery, where the legal issues were argued.

In theory copyhold estates were not subject to common law, but to the customs of the manor. However from the sixteenth century many copyholds were converted to freeholds[12] or to leases by indenture[13] and common law was assumed to apply unless it could be proved to the contrary.

Tenure under common law may be considered as freehold and was, in medieval times, divided into two main types: that held by knight service (military service) and that held by socage, or agricultural service. In the course of time the need for knight service declined and it was usually commuted to cash payment. Socage tenure was the more common form, but both forms were abolished with feudalism in 1660.

The first entry in the notebook of a nineteenth century steward to Earl Spencer is entitled *The Lawyers declaration*, it reads:

> Fee simple and a simple Fee
> And all the Fees in Tail
> Are nothing when compared with thee
> Thou best of Fees, Female.

A fee is land or freehold property which could be inherited. In common law, a fee simple estate passed to the lawful heir without restraint. The inheritance could descend to issue, but, until the Inheritance Act of 1833, could not ascend to an ancestor – such as the father or aunt.[14] Male issue was admitted before female; when there were two or more males then the eldest inherited. If there was no male and more than one female heir, the females inherited jointly as co-parceners. If there was no heir then the tenancy escheated to the lord.

Fee tail was a conditional fee which could not be alienated. It normally restricted inheritance to a direct descendant (son, granddaughter), but not collaterals such as a brother or cousin. If there were no heirs the estate reverted to the donor (or his heirs). Occasionally qualified tail, such as tail-male or tail-female may be encountered.[15]

Before 1540 real estate could not be disposed of by will.[16] After that date only freehold land could be devised directly, but by surrender to the use of a will, customary land could be, in effect, bequeathed. From 1815 copyhold land could also be disposed of by will without restriction.

Demesne land (that part of the manor reserved to the use of the lord) when rented out by copy was at the will of the lord, but not according to the custom. These tenures were not protected by custom and, since they were not by indenture, they were not leases and hence not protected by common law either. This type of tenancy was distinguished in rentals and other surveys by such terms as 'bordland' or 'runningland'. They were mostly converted to leases for years during the sixteenth and seventeenth centuries.[17]

Military service was not normally associated with customary tenure, but in Cumberland, Westmorland, North Lancashire, North Yorkshire, Northumberland and Durham it was often found in the form of Border tenant-right. This system provided tenants with low, fixed rents, on condition that they provided armed men for a given number of days a year, as required, for service against the Scots. After the accession of James I in 1604, it fell into disuse (it was discontinued on Crown manors in 1620)[18] and, being part of the feudal system, was totally abolished in 1660, although it was the basis of a number of disputes in Chancery and other civil courts over the next hundred years or so.

On many manors both freehold and customary tenants could sublet their estates, either as a whole or in part.[19] Therein lies a problem for family historians, since the under-tenants of free-holders rarely appear in the records (unless they were in trouble). For instance, Plate I lists all the freeholders of the manor of Beetham in Westmorland in 1736.[20] It is difficult to imagine Viscount Lonsdale actually ploughing the fields of his freeholding, although his estate records may provide information on who did. On many manors a customary tenant required a licence to sublet, so subtenants may be recorded in the court rolls, although not necessarily in lists of tenants such as call books and rentals.[21] A clue that subletting may have occurred would be an entry such as 'tenants of Moore' in a rental, or in a parish rate assessment.

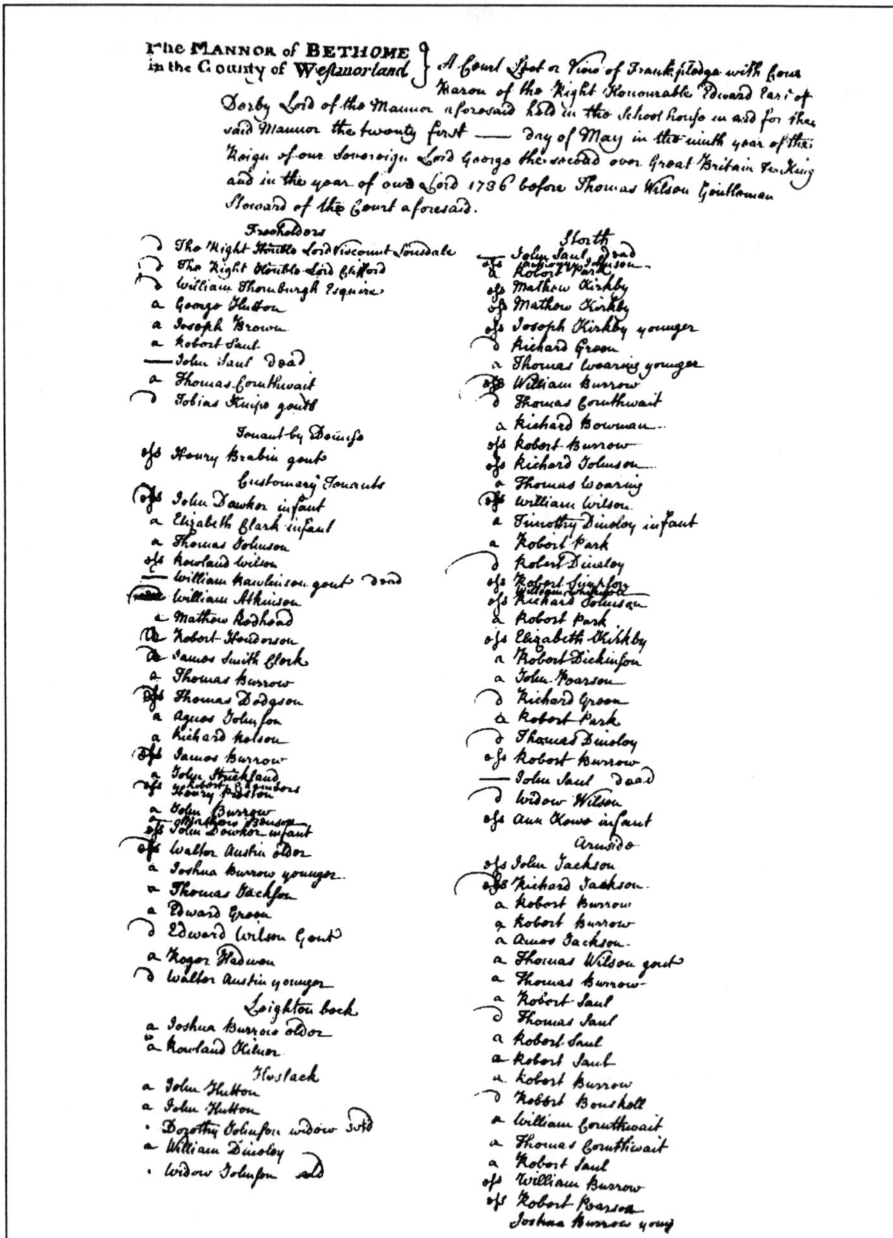

The MANNOR of BETHOME
in the County of Westmorland } A Court Leet or View of Frankpledge with Court Baron of the Right Honourable Edward Earl of Derby Lord of the Mannor aforesaid held in the School house in and for the said Mannor the twenty first — day of May in the ninth year of the Reign of our Sovereign Lord George the second over Great Britain &c King and in the year of our Lord 1736 before Thomas Wilson Gentleman Steward of the Court aforesaid.

Freeholders
d The Right Honble Lord Viscount Lonsdale
d The Right Honble Lord Clifford
d William Thornburgh Esquire
a George Hutton
a Joseph Brown
a Robert Saul
— John Saul dead
a Thomas Cowthwait
d Tobias Knipe gent

Tenant by Demise
ofs Henry Brabin gent

Customary Tenants
ofs John Dawker infant
a Elizabeth Clark infant
a Thomas Johnson
ofs Rowland Wilson
— William Rawlinson gent dead
William Atkinson
a Mathew Rodhead
Robert Henderson
James Smith Clerk
a Thomas Burrow
ofs Thomas Dodgson
a Agnes Johnson
a Richard Nelson
ofs James Burrow
a John Strickland
ofs Henry Preston / Robert Sanders
a John Burrow
a Mathew Benson
ofs John Dawker infant
ofs Walter Austin elder
a Joshua Burrow younger
a Thomas Jackson
a Edward Green
d Edward Wilson Gent
a Roger Hadwen
d Walter Austin younger

Leighton beck
a Joshua Burrow elder
a Rowland Kilner

Haslack
a John Hutton
a John Hutton
· Dorothy Johnson widow sold
a William Dinsley
· Widow Johnson sold

Storth
ofs John Saul dead / Anthony Wilkinson
a Robert Park
ofs Mathew Kirkby
ofs Mathew Kirkby
ofs Joseph Kirkby younger
d Richard Green
a Thomas Wearing younger
ofs William Burrow
d Thomas Cowthwait
a Richard Bowman
ofs Robert Burrow
ofs Richard Johnson
a Thomas Wearing
ofs William Wilson
a Timothy Dinsley infant
a Robert Park
d Robert Dinsley
ofs Robert Simpson / William Wilkinson
ofs Richard Johnson
a Robert Park
ofs Elizabeth Kirkby
a Robert Dickinson
a John Pearson
d Richard Green
a Robert Park
d Thomas Dinsley
ofs Robert Burrow
— John Saul dead
d Widow Wilson
ofs Ann Howe infant

Arnside
ofs John Jackson
ofs Richard Jackson
a Robert Burrow
a Robert Burrow
a Amos Jackson
a Thomas Wilson gent
a Thomas Burrow
a Robert Saul
d Thomas Saul
a Robert Saul
a Robert Saul
a Robert Burrow
d Robert Bousfell
a William Cowthwait
a Thomas Cowthwait
a Robert Saul
ofs William Burrow
ofs Robert Pearson
Joshua Burrow young

Plate I. *Manor of Beetham, Westmorland, 21 May 1736. Page from the court book, showing the heading and a list of tenants with notes of those who defaulted, answered or were essoined.*

CUSTOMS OF THE MANOR

As we have seen, most land tenure was dependent on the 'customs of the manor' and this, or the phrase 'according to the custom', is found time and time again in manorial records. Figure 2 is a transcript of part of a steward's notebook. It is not dated, but internal evidence suggests that it is mid-nineteenth century. In it, the steward made notes of those customs which he needed at his fingertips during a manor court hearing (he had also pasted into it newspaper reports on Chancery cases relating to tenancies). Some of the notes are referenced to precedents in the manor court books.

The transcript shows the customs of six manors – Wimbledon, Battersea and Wandsworth, Alfarthing, Down, Byfleet and Walton Leigh, all in Surrey. Earl Spencer was the lord. Under each manor are four headings: 'Heir', 'Fine', 'Dower' and 'Heriot'.

An heir was clearly defined by the common law canons of descent; the search for a man's heir went successively through all living persons who were descended from him. Only if there were no children, grandchildren or other direct descendants were brothers or cousins considered. Collaterals on the father's side were preferred to those on the mother's side. If the land came from the father's side then the mother's side was excluded and *vice versa*. Males were preferred to females of the same degree, but a woman was not excluded and could inherit in the absence of a male, for instance a man's daughter or daughters would have preference over his brother.[22] In the absence of an heir the land would escheat (revert to the lord – this could also happen if the tenant was found guilty of a felony). If an ancestor died seised of an inheritable copyhold estate then the heir's common law right was absolute. Neither a will nor the lord could disinherit him. On the other hand if the ancestor had alienated the estate in his lifetime, then the heir could claim nothing.[23]

Of the six manors, primogeniture (where the eldest son was the customary heir) was practised only at Byfleet. If there was no son, but there was more than one daughter, the estate was shared equally between them. In the other five manors the custom was that known as Borough English, where the heir was the youngest son. If there was no son in Battersea and Wandsworth the estate was to be divided among all the daughters. This is unusual since, normally under Borough English, where there was no son then the youngest daughter alone was the heir.[24] Although tenancies involving military service were inherited by the eldest son and primogeniture was normal under the common law, the tenant still had a say in the allotment of the tenancy after his death. He could grant some land as marriage portions to his daughters or alienate parts to other children, so that the heir was only entitled to the residue.[25]

Customs of Manors

Wimbledon

Heir	The Youngest son and if no Son youngest Daur' is heir to the ancestor.
Fine	Every customary Tenant shall at his first entry pay a fine if a purchaser and a relief if an Heir.
Heriot	The best beast.
Dower	The Wives shall be endowed after the death of their Husbands in the 3d part of lands according to the custom of the Common Law.

Battersea & Wandsworth

Heir	Youngest Son and in default of Son then to all the Daurs' then to youngest Brother.'
Fine	2 years on death & 1&1/2 on alienation.
Heriot	The best beast.
	Wives of Tenants dowable & shod join the son.

Alfarthing

Heir	Youngest son but in default of son all the daurs' equally. This custom also extends to collaterals vide last C.B. p1 see Ct Roll 8 June 1781.
Dower	Wife dowable.
Fine	Same as Battersea.

Down

Heir	Youngest son.
Dower	Wife Dowable.
Fine	Same as Battersea.

* Note in Battersea the youngest Son of the youngest Brother is heir in preference to the elder son of the same brother and Justably in the preference to any of his uncles fine expectations. See C.B.7. Page 116.

Byfleet

Heir	Eldest Son in default of son the eldest Daur.
Dower	Widows of Tenants dyd seized entitled to 1/3d.
Fine	2 Years on death or 1 1/2 on alienation.
Heriot	Best Beast.
Timber	The Lord entitled to one 3d of the Oak Timber.

Walton Leigh (Whole entry deleted)

Heir	Youngest Son
Dower	Widow of a tenent dyd siezed entitled to Freebench She is admitted on her husbands death.
Fine	2 year 1 1/2
Heriot	Best Beast.

Figure 2. Earl Spencer's manors, Surrey, nineteenth century: transcript of entries in a steward's notebook (Surrey Record Office: 174/4/1i).

Partibility or gavelkind (division of an estate between all sons) was common in Saxon England. Generally, it failed to survive the Middle Ages except in a few manors in Kent, where it lasted until 1926, when inheritance as a principle of succession was abolished. Its survival in Kent is attributed to the county's strategic and economic importance, which gave its population power to resist the imposition of common law.[26]

On some manors tenancies were not hereditary, but were for terms of lives. This was especially prevalent in the west of England; it was also widely used by corporate bodies such as university colleges, guilds and ecclesiastical corporations. Typically for three lives, renewal was by addition or substitution of a new life.[27] It was necessarily copyhold, since each tenancy was individually negotiated, and usually subject to arbitrary fines.

Figure 1 shows the admission of Charles Blake and his sons Samuel and William to a messuage and tenement with garden and orchard. The tenure continued until the last of them died. It was not unknown for parents to name all their children after themselves in order to slip extra lives into a tenancy of this kind, thus avoiding the expense of a new lease. In Keevil this was pre-empted by including the ages and relationships of Charles and his sons in the court record.

In manorial terms a fine was not a penalty for wrongful behaviour, but a charge paid to the lord by an incoming tenant. It would be paid if a tenant sold his tenure to another, or when a tenant died and his heir was admitted. A general fine was payable on the death of the lord. Fines might be certain (fixed) according to the custom or be arbitrary. Arbitrary fines were agreed between the lord and the new tenant, but they had to be reasonable – and were subject to acceptance by the affeerors (assessors) at the court baron before the tenant could be admitted. By the late sixteenth century arbitrary fines were being converted to certain fines. This was usually as the result of an agreement between the lord and the customary tenants and the change in custom may have been ratified by a fictitious action in Chancery.[28]

On the six manors the fine, except at Wimbledon (for which it was not given), was two years rent in the case of an heir and one-and-a-half years in the case of alienation (sale) of a tenement. On the manor of Torver in Lancashire the fines were twice the rent irrespective of whether the incoming tenant was an heir or had bought the tenancy. On the adjacent manor of Coniston, the fine for inheritance was one-and-a-half times the rent, but a new tenant could pay in excess of twenty times.[29]

A widow could not be a close blood relation of her late husband, so she was unlikely to inherit as his heir. She was, however, entitled to dower, which in common law was one third of the estate, for the remainder of her life. Where there was a joint tenancy, such as a man and his son, then the widow of a partner was not entitled to dower. Dower was often qualified by custom – the most usual being that she remain chaste or unmarried. Wills sometimes state that a wife is to enjoy use or benefits of the whole of her late husband's estate for the rest of her natural life, before it passes on to his heir.

There was some variation of dower customs in the six manors: at Walton Leigh the widow was admitted on her husband's death to the whole of the property. In this manor it was called freebench. At Battersea and Wandsworth the widow shared the tenure with the son as the heir at law.

Since a married woman could not be a tenant, her husband held the tenancy 'in the right of his wife'. On her death the tenancy passed to her heir (who in most cases was probably also her husband's), but the widower was entitled to 'Curtesy of England' which gave him the use of her estate for life. A pre-requisite of Curtesy was that the couple should have had a joint heir.

It appears that a man could alienate land directly to his wife,[30] but that she could not transfer her land directly to him; he was the tenant (albeit in his wife's right) and so could not alienate to himself. However there was a way round the problem: the couple jointly alienated the holding to a third party, who immediately alienated it back to the husband alone; it was essential to have a trustworthy intermediary!

In three of the six manors the heriot on the death of a tenant was the 'Best beast', but in Byfleet one third of all oak timber was required as well; for the remaining two manors (Down and Alfarthing) no heriot is mentioned in the notes.

As can be seen, there were differences in the customs of tenure of the six manors which were all in Surrey and with the same lord. Larger variations can be expected between regions with different agricultural practices and cultural traditions. It is therefore important to find out what the customs of your ancestors' manor were, in order that as much as possible can be gleaned from the records.

Where are the customs of 'your' manor to be found? The custumal, which, as well as outlining customs of tenure, such as those we have just seen, will give details of the services due from the tenants, the obligations of the lord and the rights of the tenants. They were drawn up from time to time, often when a new lord took over. Sometimes customs appear in the court rolls when clarification of a point was needed – two or three of the oldest inhabitants would swear that certain activities had always been done in a particular manner:

> We ordin that the water in the medow gart under the cragg shall goe where it goeth now as it apears by the Evident of Alice Gardner and James Croudson for the sayeth the hath seen it go there three scor years ago.[31]

Custumals are often found with the other manorial documents or estate papers, but copies can also turn up among the papers of Enclosure Awards. The Appendix is a transcript of parts of custumals for the manor of Walton on Thames in 1725 and 1728. It shows the tenants' rights-of-use on the common or waste of the manor and was presented as evidence of land use in an Enclosure Award hearing in 1796. The customs of many manors have been published at various times by individual antiquaries and by county record and antiquarian societies and, in part, in older volumes of the *Victoria County History* series.

THE RECORDS

In a study carried out on a random sample of manors from Sussex, Oxfordshire, Huntingdonshire, Wiltshire and Westmorland, Anita Travers showed that for about one third of manors only the name is known – there are no documents. Less than a fifth have a good run of records from the sixteenth or seventeenth centuries and only one in twenty-five has a good run from before this.[32] Having said this, there should be records for over half of the manors for the eighteenth, nineteenth and early twentieth centuries.

The earliest records are from the thirteenth century. Before about 1540 all documents produced by the estate management process are classed as manorial records. Afterwards only the proceedings of the courts are regarded as such; the other material being classed as Estate papers.[33] The records belong to the lord of the manor under whom they were created – they are not part of the manor, hence the custumal on the change of lord. Since they were not part of the manor they were liable to remain in the possession of the old lord and so are often dispersed in private hands.

Court rolls

In medieval times the minutes of the proceedings of the manorial courts were written on parchment membranes which were sewn together to form a long strip which was rolled up for storage. Hence they are normally referred to as 'court rolls', although by Tudor times they were often written on paper and bound in book form.

Before 1734, except for the Commonwealth period, (1653-1660), the law required all legal records to be in Latin, but a great many manorial records are, however, in English.[34] Ecclesiastical manor rolls are usually in Latin right up to 1734.

However, even when the documents are in Latin, the format is stylised and by familiarising yourself with the layout and terminology from later records, you should be able to cope. In addition the clerks in many manors were not Latin scholars and tended to write much in English and only latinized such things as names or standard phrases. In fact the handwriting may present greater problems (see Plates IX, X and X1), although in theory it was meant to be in a legible court hand. Two useful books are: *Latin for Local History* by Eileen Gooder and Jane Morris' *A Latin Glossary for Family and Local History*.

Some time before the date of the court the lord's steward instructed the bailiff to give public notice to the tenants and other interested parties and command them to attend. He was also to summon the jury or homage. The court was often held on a particular day, such as the third Friday in October, but special courts could be held to deal with specific items.

The steward (or his deputy) presided over the court in the same way as a judge. Whatever the local variations in the manor or its customs, the courts were all conducted on similar lines – the stewards used the same handbooks and applied the same common law.

At the appointed time, the steward entered the court which was called to order by the bailiff. The clerk wrote the heading in the (draft) minute book – we have already seen a typical heading in Figure 1 – giving the name of the manor, the style of the court, the name of the lord, the date the court was held and who presided. Sometimes the name of the clerk would also be given.

A roll call was taken of the tenants, those absent, or defaulting, were amerced, but those with a valid excuse (essoin) were let off with a nominal payment. Plate I is from the Court Book of Beetham in Westmorland for the year 1736.[35] The page contains a list of names of tenants who owed suit to the court – first all the freeholders, then a tenant by demise (lease of desmene land)[36] followed by the customary tenants.

Each name on the list has been annotated: 'd' for default, 'a' for answered (attended court) and 'ess' for essoin – note the long 's'. A number of tenants are marked as 'dead', so comparison with the list and date of the last court could give a clue to date of death. This is useful if the parish registers are incomplete or the tenant was buried outside the parish; it can also help distinguish a child from an adult when, as is frequent, ages are not given in the burial register. Several tenants are identified as 'dead'. The first 'dead' tenant is a freeholder John Saul; it is apparent, from the tenants of the township of Storth, that he also held two customary tenures. Immediately below John Saul is another freehold tenant, Thomas Cornthwaite; in the listing, again under Storth, there is a customary tenant Thomas Cornthwaite; it is tempting to assume that they are one and the

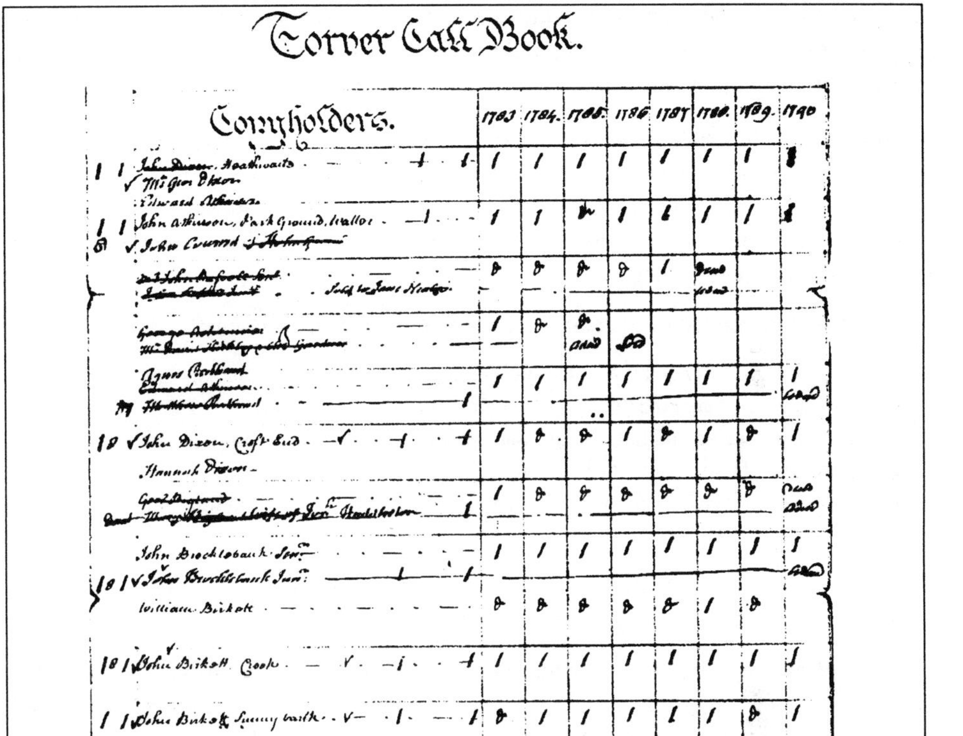
Torver Call Book.

Copyholders. 1783 1784 1785 1786 1787 1788 1789 1790

John Dixon, Heathwaite
John Brocklebank Senr.
John Brocklebank Junr.
William Birkett
Thomas Bell
John Gawith
Thomas Dixon

Plate II. *Manor of Torver in Lancashire, 1799-1817. Call book – looking much like a school register. The names of tenants who died or alienated are crossed out and replaced by those of the new tenants.*

same, but the freeholder answered while the customary tenant defaulted. Looking further down another Thomas Cornthwaite, of Arnside, did answer – he *may* be the freeholder. It is evident then, that there were at least two tenants called Thomas Cornthwaite.

By the eighteenth century call books were often used; they were registers that were called out at the court (Plate II).[37] The books usually covered several years and changes in the tenantry were noted down in them. After the roll call the steward called the jury or homage to attention and swore in the foreman and then the other members in groups of three or four. Plate III shows a Jury list.[38]

The jury were reminded of the courts authority and of their own duty:

> You shall diligently enquire and true presentment make of all such matters and things as shall be given in charge the Queen's councell that Followes & that owns.39 You shall well and truly keep secrett and not disclose butt by way of p'sentation. You shall not spare any p'son for your favor or affection, or present any for hathred or mallice that you bear to them, butt in all things you shall p'sent ye truth whole truth and nothing butt ye truth according to your best endivor.[40]

The jury or homage sometimes served until the following court, but it was often appointed, sworn and discharged on the same day.

The role of the jury was both inquisitorial and judicial. When the jurors were appointed they were charged to discover and present to the court all persons who had committed offences against the common good. They presented offenders of their own knowledge,

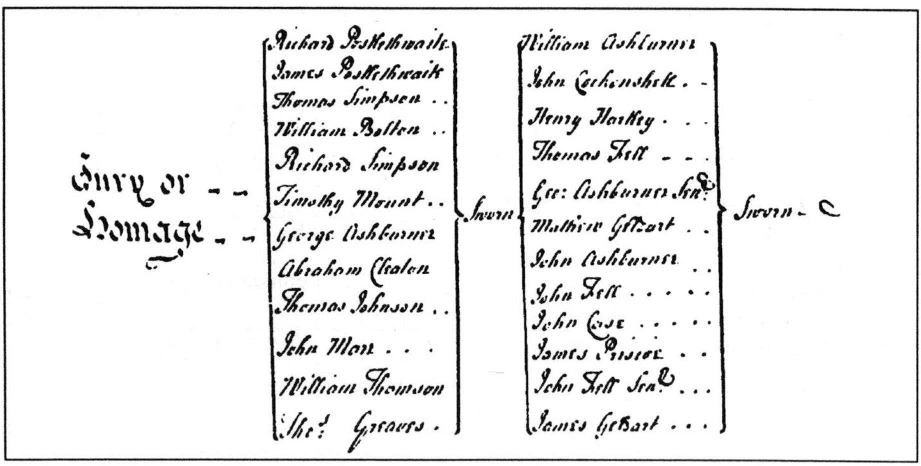
Jury or Homage – –
Richard Postlethwaite
James Postlethwaite
Thomas Simpson ..
William Bolton ..
Richard Simpson
Timothy Mount ..
George Ashburner
Abraham Chalon
Thomas Johnson ..
John Mon . . .
William Thomson
Thos Greaves .
Sworn
William Ashburner
John Cockenshell . -
Henry Harkey . . .
Thomas Fell - - .
Geo: Ashburner Junr
Matthew Gilbart . .
John Ashburner ..
John Fell . . . . .
John Cose . . . . .
James Rigg . .
John Fell Senr . . .
James Gelbart . . .
Sworn – C

***Plate III**. Manor of Muchland, Lancashire, 12 May 1742. The members of the jury or homage for the court baron. The first named, Richard Postlethwaite, was the foreman. By local custom there were twenty-four homagers for this court, the nearby manor of Torver usually had thirteen.*

aided by reports from the various court officials such as the constable, the pinder or the hedgelooker. The jury's presentment in court usually condemned defendants, even in their absence, and indicated the penalty – usually an amercement. There was no necessity to hear witnesses and only rarely was the defendant represented by attorney or counsel. The penalty was referred to the steward and affeerors for ratification. The sentence could only be reversed at the same session, at the steward's discretion, by another jury – and was not subject to appeal at another court.[41]

Following the swearing-in of the jury or homage, the list of offences which could be heard by the court – some sixty by a court leet and over forty by a court baron – was read out. Then the officials were appointed (Plate IV).

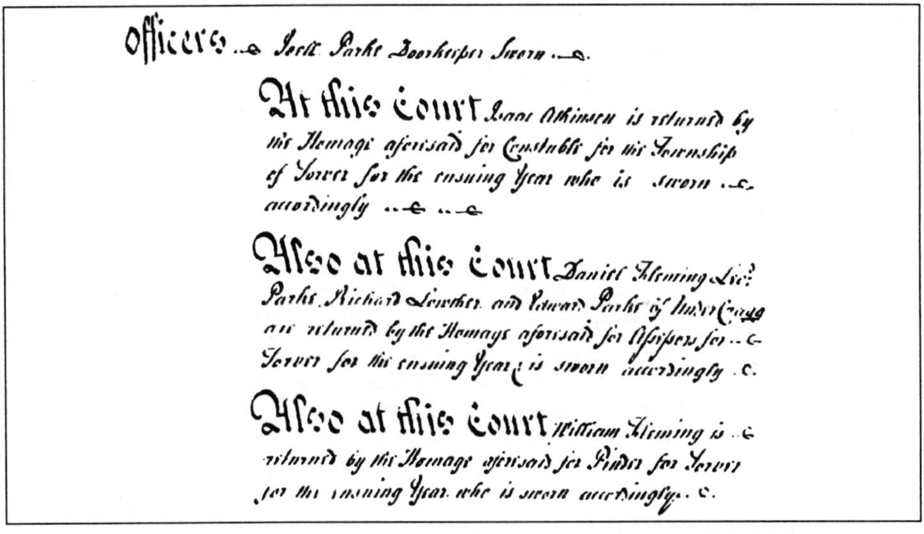

Officers ... Jereb? Parke Doorkeeper Sworn ...

At this Court Isaac Atkinson is returned by the Homage aforesaid for Constable for the Township of Torver for the ensuing Year who is sworn accordingly ...

Also at this Court Daniel Fleming Isa? Parke, Richard Lowther and Edward Parke of Undercrag are returned by the Homage aforesaid for Assessors for Torver for the ensuing Year & is sworn accordingly ...

Also at this Court William Fleming is returned by the Homage aforesaid for Pinder for Torver for the ensuing Year who is sworn accordingly ...

Plate IV*. Manor of Torver, Lancashire, 23 October 1742. Appointment of officers at the court baron.*

First the constable was sworn in:

> You shall swear to serve our soverign Lord the King in the office of Constables for the year. That you shall see that the peace of our soverign Lord the King be well & truly kept in your power, that watch & ward be kept according to the statute. You shall endeavour yourselves for the punishment of vagabonds Rogues & other who presence within your office that they be punished. You shall well & truly execute all p'cons & precepts which come to you from the justice of the peace & do your best in all after business belonging to your office without favour.[42]

Two hundred years later and two hundred miles away, the constables on Earl Spencer's six manors were being sworn-in:

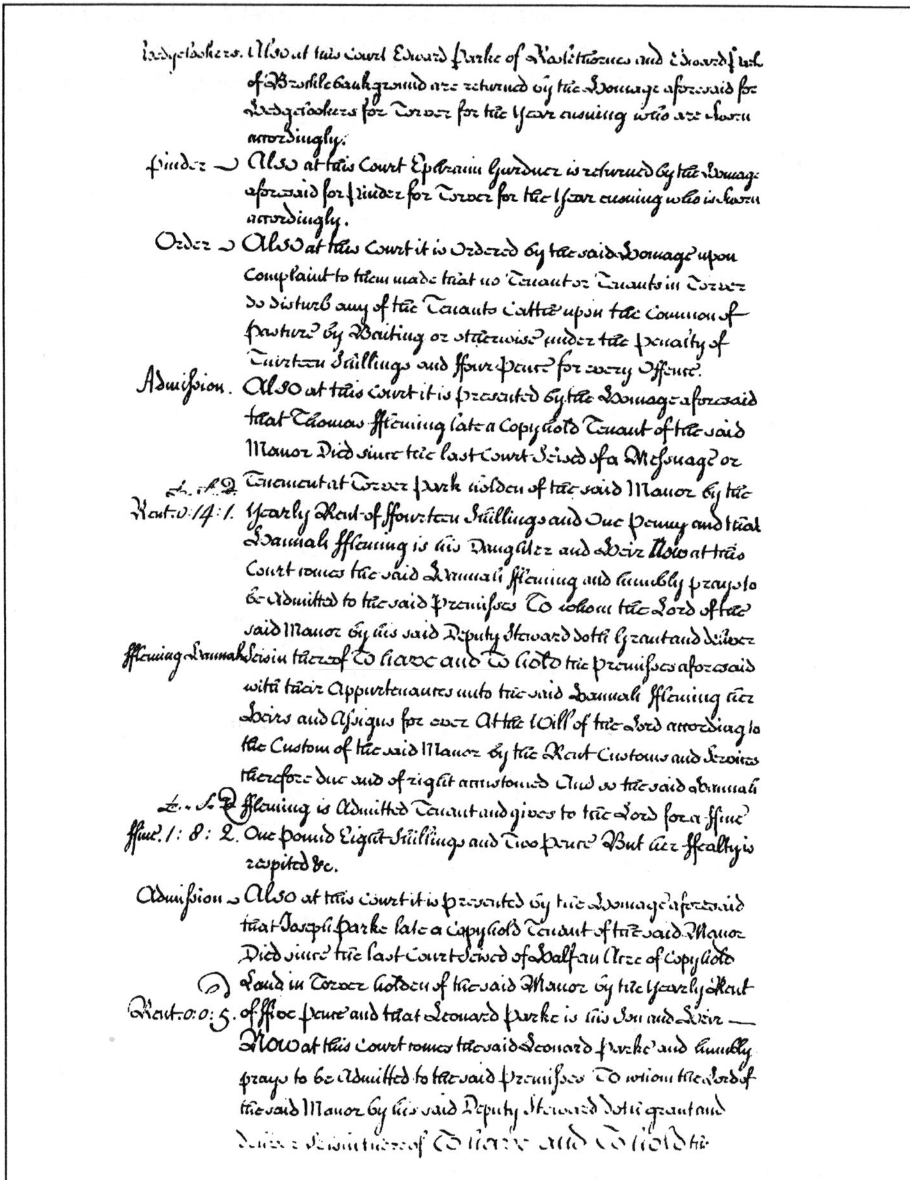
Hedgelookers. Also at this Court Edward Parke of Rosethornes and Edward Fell of Broadlebankground are returned by the Homage aforesaid for Hedgelookers for Torver for the Year ensuing who are Sworn accordingly.

Pinder — Also at this Court Ephraim Gardner is returned by the Homage aforesaid for Pinder for Torver for the Year ensuing who is Sworn accordingly.

Order — Also at this Court it is Ordered by the said Homage upon Complaint to them made that no Tenant or Tenants in Torver do disturb any of the Tenants Cattle upon the Common of Pasture by Baiting or otherwise under the Penalty of Thirteen Shillings and Four Pence for every Offence.

Admission. Also at this Court it is presented by the Homage aforesaid that Thomas ffleming late a Copyhold Tenant of the said Manor Died since the last Court Seised of a Messuage or

£. s. d. Tenement at Torver Park holden of the said Manor by the

Rent. 0: 14: 1. Yearly Rent of ffourteen Shillings and One Penny and that Hannah ffleming is his Daughter and Heir Now at this Court comes the said Hannah ffleming and humbly prays to be Admitted to the said Premises To whom the Lord of the said Manor by his said Deputy Steward doth Grant and deliver

ffleming Hannah Seisin thereof To have and to hold the Premises aforesaid with their Appurtenances unto the said Hannah ffleming her Heirs and Assigns for ever At the Will of the Lord according to the Custom of the said Manor by the Rent Customs and Services therefore due and of right accustomed And so the said Hannah

£. s. d. ffleming is Admitted Tenant and gives to the Lord for a ffine

ffine. 1: 8: 2. One Pound Eight Shillings and Two Pence But her ffealty is respited &c.

Admission — Also at this Court it is presented by the Homage aforesaid that Joseph Parke late a Copyhold Tenant of the said Manor Died since the last Court Seised of Half an Acre of Copyhold

(d) Land in Torver holden of the said Manor by the Yearly Rent

Rent. 0: 0: 5. of ffive Pence and that Leonard Parke is his Son and Heir — Now at this Court comes the said Leonard Parke and humbly prays to be Admitted to the said Premises To whom the Lord of the said Manor by his said Deputy Steward doth grant and deliver Seisin thereof To have and to hold the

***Plate V**. Manor of Torver, Lancashire, 23 October 1741. Extract from the court proceedings, showing the layout of a typical page. Note the wide left hand margin in which the nature of the business (order, admission etc.), the name of the principal party, rent and fine are shown for ease of reference.*

> You shall well and truly swear by our Sovereign Lord the King & the Lord of this Leet in the Office of Constable or Headborough in and for the Manor of Betsey until you are thence discharged by due course of Law – You shall well and truly do & execute all things to your office according to the best of your state and knowledge – So hold you to God.

After the constable(s) the various minor officials took their oaths. Plate IV shows: assessors (affeerors) who assessed fines and amercements meted out by the jury, one of whom is identified by his abode – suggesting that there was more than one man of that name on the manor; pinders who rounded up any stray animals. Service as a court-appointed officer was compulsory for all adult males on the manor and could be enforced by amercement or distraint of goods by the bailiff.

Those not wishing to take their turn might, if they could afford to, pay a surrogate to carry out their duties. Each officer was responsible for presenting offences that fell within the jurisdiction of his office to the jury. Their reports have sometimes survived, but on too many occasions they only say *omni bene* – all is well.

Records of payments to officers of the courts are rare, but there is evidence that they did receive some compensation for their inconvenience. There may be references to parcels of land such as 'Constables Acre' or 'Reevewick Lands' which were held for the year by those in office.[43] At Walton on Thames in Surrey the pinders were paid so much per head for the strays they impounded (see Appendix).

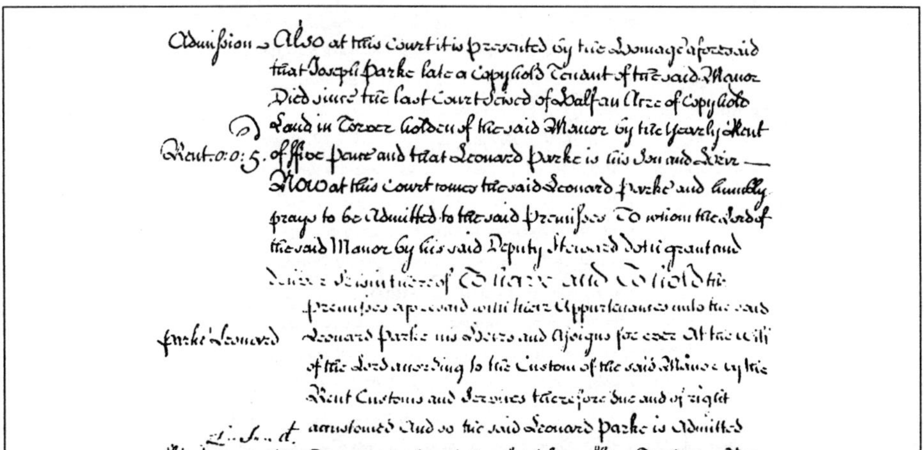
Admission – Also at this Court it is presented by the Homage aforesaid that Joseph Parke late a Copyhold Tenant of the said Manor Died since the last Court seized of Half an Acre of Copyhold (2) Land in Torver holden of the said Manor by the yearly Rent Rent 0:0:5. of five pence and that Leonard Parke is his Son and Heir — Now at this Court comes the said Leonard Parke and humbly prays to be Admitted to the said Premises To whom the Lord of the said Manor by his said Deputy Steward doth grant and deliver Seisin thereof To have and to hold the premises aforesaid with their Appurtenances unto the said Parke Leonard Leonard Parke his Heirs and Assigns for ever At the Will of the Lord according to the Custom of the said Manor by the Rent Customs and Services therefore due and of right £ s d accustomed And so the said Leonard Parke is Admitted Fine 0:0:10 Tenant and gives to the Lord for a Fine Ten pence But his fealty is respited &c.

Plate VI*. Manor of Torver, Lancashire, 23 October 1741. This extract from the court baron minutes records the admission of Leonard Parke to his late father's tenement.*

The business of the court continued (Plate V) with an order from the homage that, as the result of a complaint, in future anyone found guilty of disturbing or baiting the cattle grazing on the common would be amerced 13s 4d.[44] Orders such as this were made by the jury regarding a range of estate and agricultural matters, including keeping water courses in order, making the highway (if not taken over by the parish), public nuisance (such as the siting of dunghills close to a neighbour's house), keeping houses habitable (they were the property of the lord), right of way and access. Apart from general orders, such as is illustrated in Plate V, there may be specific presentments naming individuals:

> p'sent Jo: Atkinson & Aster Asburner for not making hedge Against payne of either of them vjd

> p'sent Ric: Croudson for not making his watter race in the
> beckmedow Against payne ijs vjd

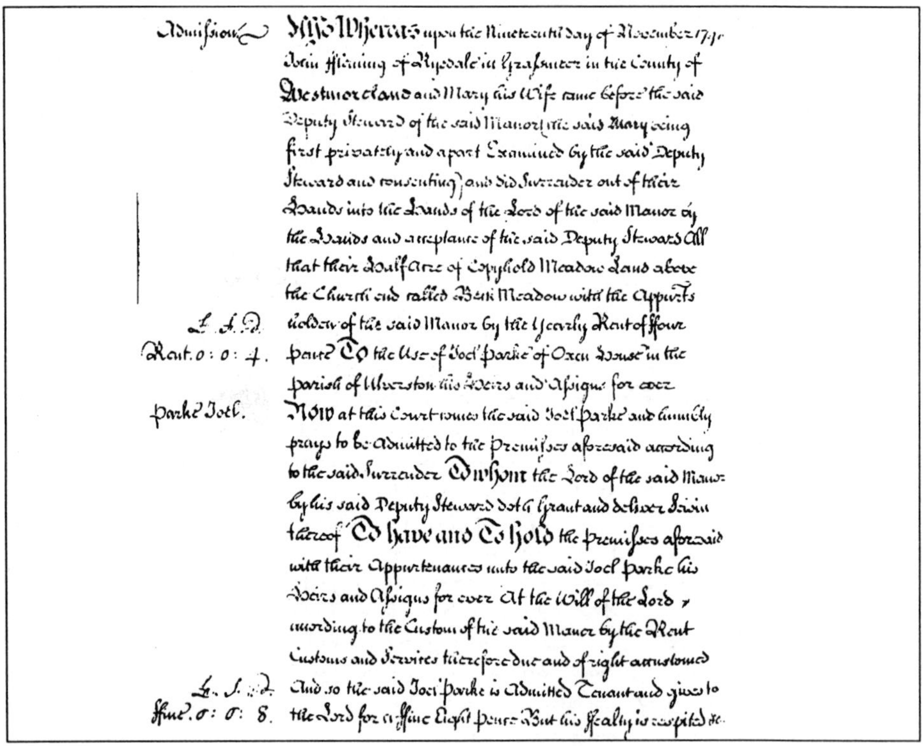

Admission — Whereas upon the Nineteenth day of November 1741 John ffleming of Rydale in Grasmere in the County of Westmorland and Mary his Wife came before the said Deputy Steward of the said Manor (the said Mary being first privately and apart Examined by the said Deputy Steward and consenting) and did Surrender out of their hands into the hands of the Lord of the said Manor by the hands and acceptance of the said Deputy Steward All that their halfe Acre of Copyhold Meadow Land above the Church end called Beck Meadow with the Appurts holden of the said Manor by the yearly Rent of ffour

£. s. d.
Rent. 0: 0: 4. pence To the Use of Joel Parke of Oxen House in the parish of Ulverston his Heirs and Assigns for ever

Parke Joel. Now at this Court comes the said Joel Parke and humbly prays to be Admitted to the Premisses aforesaid according to the said Surrender Whom the Lord of the said Manor by his said Deputy Steward doth Grant and deliver Seisin thereof To have and To hold the Premisses aforesaid with their Appurtenances unto the said Joel Parke his Heirs and Assigns for ever At the Will of the Lord according to the Custom of the said Manor by the Rent Customs and Services therefore due and of right accustomed

£. s. d.
ffine. 0: 0: 8. And so the said Joel Parke is Admitted Tenant and gives to the Lord for a ffine Eight pence But his ffealty is respited &c.

***Plate VII**. Manor of Torver, Lancashire, 23 October 1741. Admission of Joel Parke after alienation by John and Mary Fleming. Mary had inherited the land, although John was the tenant 'in the right of his wife'. See also Plate VIII.*

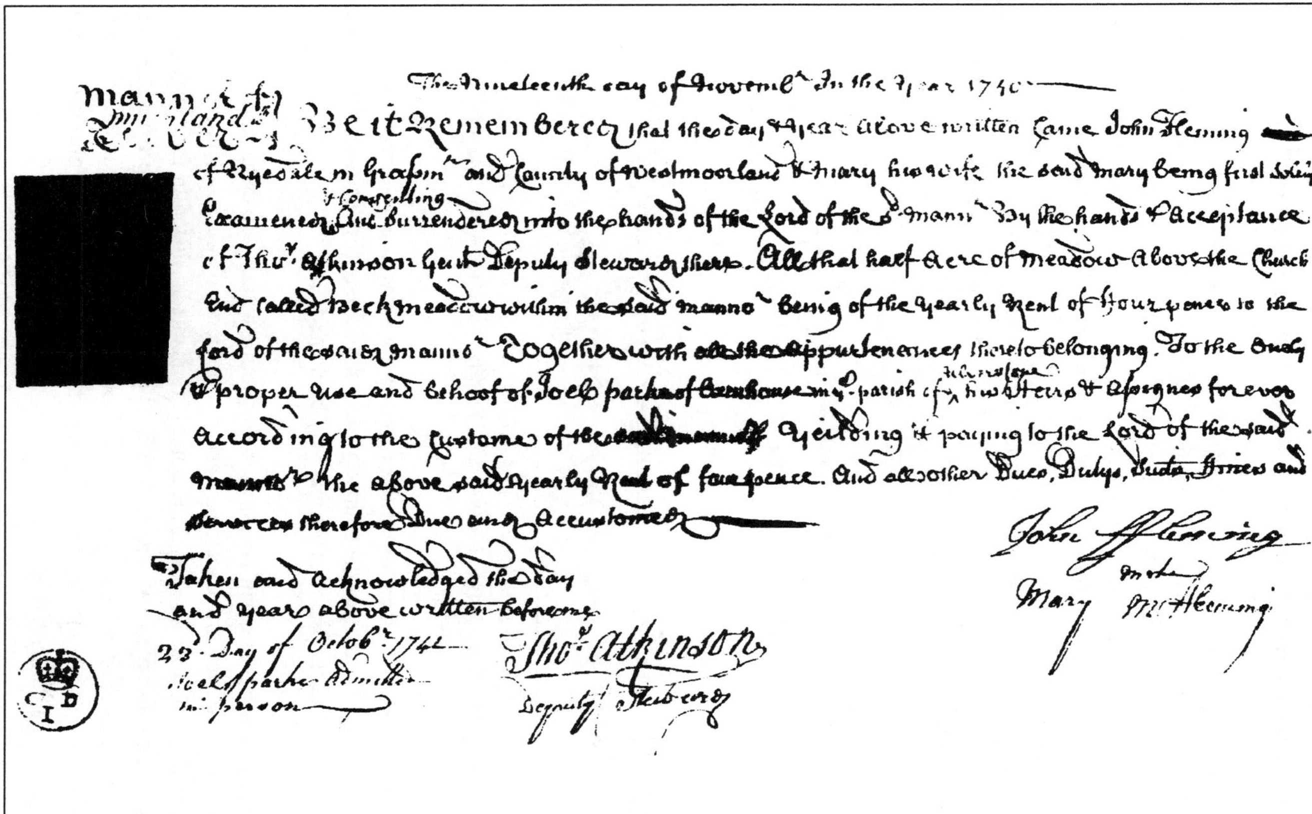

The Nineteenth day of Novemb[r] In the year 1740

Be it Remembered that the day & year above written Came John Fleming of Ryedale in Grasm[ere] and County of Westmoorland & Mary his wife the said Mary being first soly examined And surrendered into the hands of the Lord of the s[d] mann[r] By the hands & Acceptance of Tho[s] Atkinson Gent Deputy Steward there. All that half Acre of Meadow Above the Church End called Beckmeadow within the said mannor Being of the yearly Rent of Fourpence to the Lord of the said mannor Together with all the Appurtenances thereto belonging. To the Only proper use and behoof of Joel parke of Oxenhouse in y[e] parish of Ulverstone his Heirs & Assignes for ever According to the Custome of the said mannor Yeilding & paying to the Lord of the said mannor the above said yearly Rent of fourpence. And all other Dues, Dutys, Suits, Fines and Services therefore Dues and Accustomed

John Fleming

Mary (mark) Fleming

Taken and Acknowledged the Day and year above written before me

Tho[s] Atkinson

Deputy Steward

23 Day of Octob[r] 1741

Joel Parke Admitted in person

Plate VIII. *Manor of Torver, Lancashire, 19 November 1740. Surrender by John and Mary Fleming of land to 'the use and behoof' of Joel Parke of Oxenhouse in the parish of Ulverston. In the bottom left-hand corner is a note that Joel was admitted at the next court baron (see Plate VII). It is interesting to note that the surrender was made the day that Mary was admitted to the tenement.*

p'sent the howses at undercrag of William Wilson decayed and we order that the said howses shal be mended and full before the next court upon payne of vjs viijd[45]

Following the order in Plate V is an admission: the homage presented that Thomas Fleming was dead and that Hannah his daughter was his heir.[46] Thomas was a copyholder of a messuage and tenement at a rent of 14s. 1d. We can look in the parish registers for Thomas's burial where we find he was of Torver Park – presumably the site of his tenement. From the registers we can also find that Thomas had married Mary Brown in 1736 and that Hannah was only a year old. Hannah, or rather her representative, asked to be admitted to her father's tenure and seisin was granted to her and her heirs and assignees for ever – not for lives. At the end we see that Hannah paid a fine of £1 8s. 2d. – twice the rent.

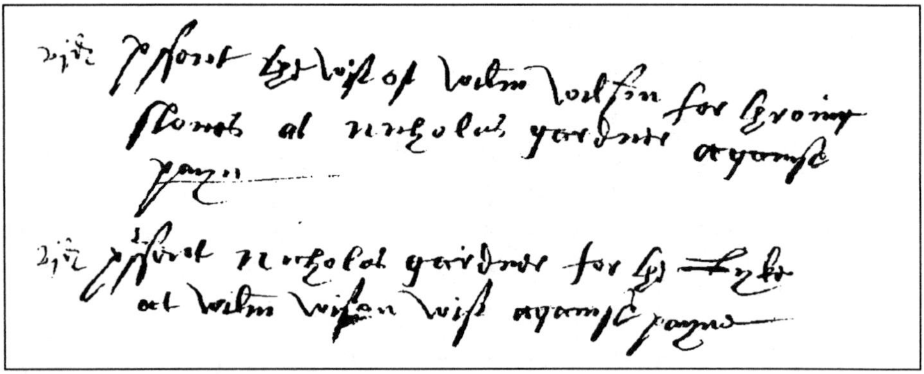

Plate IX. *Manor of Torver, Lancashire, 4 August 1640. Court leet presentments by the homage in English. William Wilson's wife and Nicholas Gardner were amerced 6d each for throwing stones at each other.*

Entries frequently give the location of the property by mentioning adjacent holdings. Many court rolls give the date of the court at which an outgoing (or deceased) tenant was admitted and occasionally previous tenants may be named.

In the left hand margin is Hannah's name as the incoming tenant – this was made for ease of reference for the steward checking back on holders of the land, but it is also useful to family historians. At Keevil the outgoing tenants are listed in the margin, this is not quite so helpful unless, as occurred at Keevil, the names of the previous tenants are given in the text. Some court books are indexed, either integrally, or in a separate volume. These indexes usually list incoming tenants, but this should be checked, it may be the outgoing tenants that are indexed.

Plate VI shows the admission of Leonard Parke following the death of his father Joseph. Leonard was heir to half an acre, rent 5d. Joseph appears to have been a poor man – no messuage is mentioned. He seems to have scrabbled a living out of half an acre and was probably employed as an agricultural labourer or in the local woollen industry. Again, researchers should not look at the records in isolation: the registers show that Joseph was 'of Stable Harvey' when Leonard was baptised in 1692, and they also show that he died there – a long time for a labourer to stay in one place. The inventory with his will substantiates this: he had £115 owing to him, he had £10 worth of sheep (80-90 – a large flock as 40-50 was the average size in this area) and £2 in wool and probably had four cattle, in total he was worth over £140. He was, in fact, a tenant of the adjacent manor of Blawith. The records of the manor of Blawith have not survived, but the deeds of Stable Harvey go back to 1624.[47] They contain many pertinent extracts from Blawith manor records, including conveyances which indicate that Joseph was a freehold tenant. Copies of surrenders may also be found among deeds, as well as will extracts and other relevant material.

Plate VII shows another admission on 23 October 1741, this time not as the result of an inheritance, but of an alienation. John Fleming of Rydal and Mary his wife had sold a tenancy to Joel Parke. Mary was examined privately by the steward to establish that she consented to the sale; this implies that she was the heir to the tenement and that John was the tenant in the right of his wife. Looking once again at the Torver registers we see that John Fleming of Grasmere, a cooper, married Mary Carter of Torver in 1721 and that in 1740 Mary's father Mathew of Torver Park had died, leaving his daughter as heir. Mary had been admitted at the court held on 19 November 1740.[48] Joel Parke paid his fine and was admitted – again the fine was twice the rent, the same as paid by an heir.

Plate VIII is the record of the surrender.[49] At alienation the land was 'surrendered into the hands of the lord ... to the use and behoof of' the new tenant. In other words, the lord held the tenancy in trust to the benefit of the incoming tenant until he was admitted at the next court baron. Between surrender and admission the incoming tenant could work the land, but not alienate or sublet it. Surrender and admission was the method of conveyance of copyhold land until 1925 when copyhold tenure was abolished.[50] Properties still held by customary tenure just before World War I may be identified in the Valuation Office field books, created under the 1910 Finance (1909-1910) Act at TNA.[51]

So far there have been no recorded offences against the law. By the eighteenth century many courts leet had wasted away; Torver was no exception and, apart from appointing the constable, the court baron was concerned solely with the administration of the manor as an estate. In the first half of the seventeenth century both courts were active

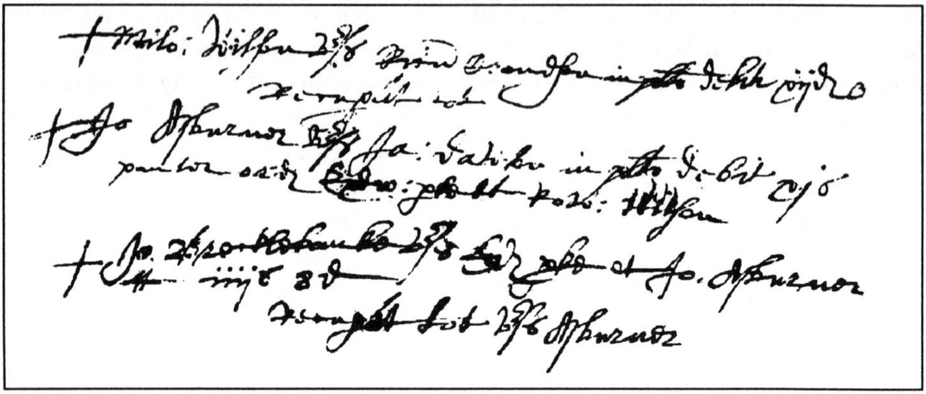

***Plate X.** Manor of Torver, Lancashire, about 1647. Court leet, three pleas of debt in Latin. The standard layout and phrasing help make them easier to follow:*
'+ Milo: Wilson vrss Ricu' Croudson in plto debiti xijd - Recupat tot (Miles Wilson against Richard Croudson in a plea of debt for 12d. Recovered in total.)
+ Jo: Asburner vrs Ja: Dawson in plto debit vjs – Poniter ord' Edw: p'ke et Row: Wilson (John Asburner against James Dawson in a plea of debt 6s. – Edward Parke and Rowland Wilson to investigate)
+ Jo Brocklebanke vrss Ed p'ke et Jo: Asburner iiijs xd – Recupat tot vrss Asburner (John Brocklebank against Edward Parke and John Asburner 4s. 10d. – Recovered in total against Asburner.)

at Torver, when a number of petty offences and private disputes were heard by them.[52] Plate IX shows a typical entry from the 1640 court leet; it is worth noting that it is written in English.[53] The presentments can often give an insight into the personalities of long dead ancestors.

On 29 September 1626 the Torver court baron heard four cases involving Katherine Wilson. In the first, Philip Addison was presented for a 'blodwick' (approximately grievous bodily harm) upon Katherine Wilson, he was found guilty and was bound over in the sum of 3s. 4d. Next, Katherine herself was presented for accusing Eliner Parke of housebreaking and stealing yarn – she was ordered to be 'stocked and confess her fault'; in the following case she was presented for calling the wife of Richard Atkinson 'that grenerig bastard' (Greenrigg was the name of Richard Atkinson's farm); finally she was presented for charging Philip Wilson 'that he pulled of hir clothes and have Ravished hir' – she was ordered to be put in the stocks for these last two offences. These four cases give us an indication of Katherine's character and suggest, perhaps, that Philip Addison may have been somewhat hard done by.[54]

At the next court, (14 October 1627) Thomas Parke was presented for calling William Atkinson a rogue, he was bound over.[55] This slander case was not as trivial as it sounds today, for, under the vagrancy laws, a rogue or vagabond could have been stripped to the waist and whipped until his back was bloodied before being sent on his way.

At the same court Margaret Askew was presented for calling Thomas Parke rogue. This was followed by the pair of them being presented 'for a fray between them' – Thomas was amerced 20d. Complementary presentments such as these are common.

At the court baron on 22 February 1631/2 Robert Place, minister, was bound over for a blodwick upon Robert Parke. Place was also presented 'for charging to Thomas Fleming that if he had not worn the coat he did (if he hadn't been the curate) he would have cutted off his ears' – against pain (bound over).[56]

At the same court, Jenat Lowther was presented and bound over for calling Thomas Parke and John Dodgson 'sheepstealer and muttoner' – no light matter at a time when sheep stealing was a capital offence.

On 8 May 1633 Robert Place and John Taylor were presented for a 'hubleshow (disturbing the peace) between them' – both amerced 3d.[57] Robert Place was also presented for calling John Atkinson, tanner, 'meansworn' (a liar) – against pain 5s. As a follow up, Place was bound over for stopping John Atkinson's workmen on his own ground.

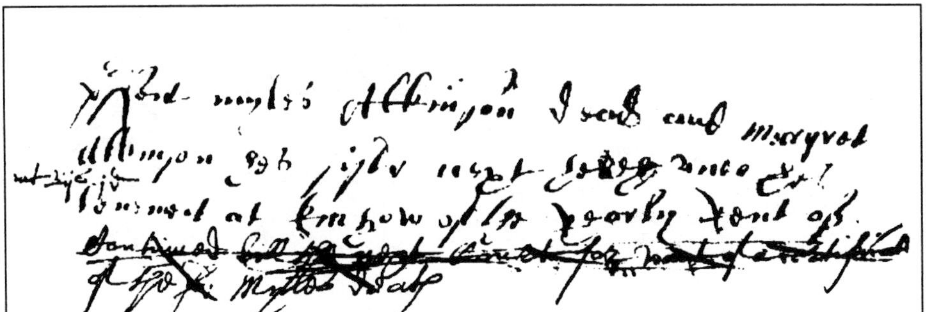

Plate XI. *Manor of Torver, Lancashire, 30th June 1641. Verdict in draft court book: 'p'sent myles Atkinson dead and Margret Atkinson, hes sister next heir unto his tenement at Emhow of the yearly Rent of.' (Underneath is a crossed out comment: 'Continued till the next Court for want of a certificate of the said Myles death')*

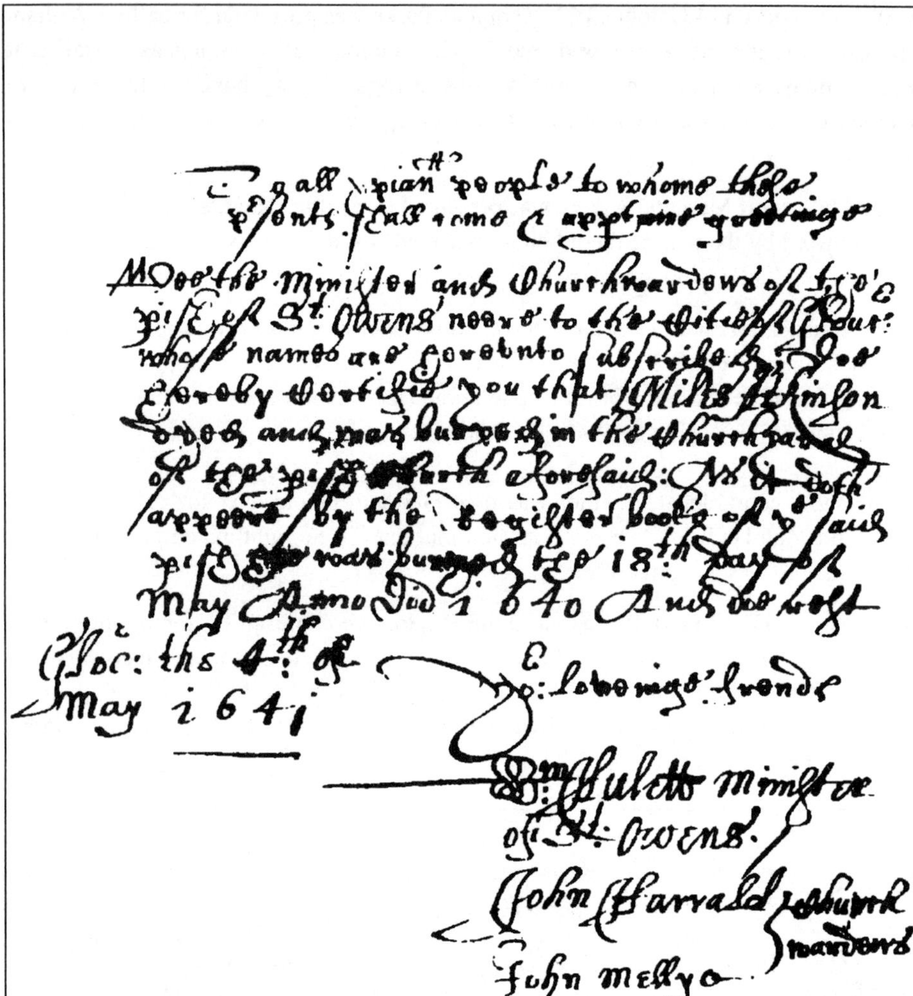

To all Christian people to whome these presents shall come & appertaine greetinge
Wee the minister and Churchwardens of the parish of St. Owens neere to the Citie of Gloucester whose names are hereunto subscribed doe hereby certifie you that Miles Atkinson dyed and was buryed in the Churchyard of the parish Church aforesaid: As it doth appeare by the register booke of ye said parish he was buryed the 18th day of May Anno Domini 1640 And soe we rest

Gloc: the 4th of May 1641

Your lovinge frends

Wm. Hulett minister of St. Owens

John Harrald Churchwardens
John Melly

Plate XII. *Manor of Torver, Lancashire. A certificate of death (dated 4 May 1641) was bound into the draft court book, next to the verdict shown in Plate XI. Without it, it is very unlikely that Myles Atkinson's migration to Gloucester would have come to light.*

Also at this court James Parke and David Fleming were presented separately for blodwicks on each other; both were bound over. The court had not finished with James Parke though, for he was presented for a blodwick upon Richard Wilson – 'against payne xxd; else to be sett in the stocks for an hour ij Sundays after evenig prayer'. Wilson was also presented for a blodwick upon Parke – 'the lyke punishment or xxd'.

Most of the Torver court leet records were written in Latin, as in Plate X (Plate IX is an exception). Cases to come before the court leet included:

22 July 1624 John Croudson against James Croudson for a debt of 22s. – recovered in total. Isabell Proctor administratix of Leonard against William Atkinson of Souterstead for a debt of 8s. – recovered 7s. 6d. [58]

13 July 1630 Robert Place, minister, was presented for beating John Wilson at the last court – against pain 12d.[59] Place was also presented for a blodwick upon Rowland Wilson in the highway; against pain. Robert Place, minister, was a very turbulent priest – his name occurs frequently in both courts, often for violent or threatening behaviour; his dispute with John Atkinson was only ended when Atkinson complained to a higher authority, the local justice of the peace.[60]

On 22 February 1631 Robert Place entered a plea of debt against Robert Parke for 20s. 10d.[61] Parke countered with a plea against Place for a debt of 18s. – Parke was awarded 23d. by the homage. Counter charges of debt such as this are common. Debts of forty shillings or more had to be heard in a higher court, and it is not unusual to find several claims for thirty-nine shillings and eleven pence three-farthings by one plaintiff against the same defendant.

While pleas of debt were heard exclusively by the court leet and pleas of slander normally by the court baron, there seems to have been some overlap in the jurisdictions of Torver's courts at this period, as both heard cases of violence.

As can be seen from Plates IX to XII, the handwriting is not the easiest at this period, but with a little perseverance it can be deciphered.

1649	**1649** *(cont)*	**1664**	**1664** *(cont)*
Wm Greaves	Robt Kendall	Tho: Atkinson	John Ashburner
John Jackson	Edw: Parke	John Addison	William Atkinson
Rodger Atkinson	Anth: Parke	Christo: Dodshon	Robt Fleigmine
Rich: Atkinson	John Croudson	Willm Dodshon	James Atkinson
Robt Atkinson	Robt Wilson	Nicolas Jackson	Rodgr Whinfield
Wm Atkinson	James Wilson	Row: Crowdson	Leo: Parke
Leonard Crowdson	Tho: Dickson	Robt Wilson	John Parke
James Crowdson	Wm Redhead	Row: Wilson	John Wennington
John Brocksbank	John Redhead	John Atkinson	Willm Atkinson
Chr: Addison	Wm Gardner	Willm Jackson	Richd Parke
Hen: Flemyng		Rich: Wilson	Tho: Dixon
Roger Atkinson		Leond Croudson	John Parke
Rich: Garner		Leond Rooke	
Wm Wilson		James Willson	
Tho: Croudson		Leo: Parke	
Robt Wilson		Robt Atkinson	
James Danson		James Parke	
John Ashburner		Row: Jackson	
John Atkinson		John Stilling	
Miles Flemynge		John Willson	
James Atkinson		Tho: Parke	
James Atkinson		Edw: Parke	
Leo: Park		Robt Parke	
Ux James Wilson		Edw: Parke	
Wm Atkinson		Myles Wilson	
John Addison		Tho: Atkinson &}	
Tho: Atkinson		Math: Lowther }	
John Park		John Croudson	
Math: Taylor		Jam: Willson	
Tho: Dodgson		Elenor Jackson	
Wm Harrison		Robt Gruaves	
Tho: Wilson		Row: Atkinson	
Rowland Wilson		Willm Atkinson	
John Atkinson		Robt Atkinson	
Edw: Richardson		Willm Atkinson	
Rich: Brocksbank		Rich: Atkinson	
John Crowdson		Leo: Croudson	
Leonard Rooke		Rich: Croudson	
Wm Dickson		Willm Dixon	
Robt Addison		Ja: Brocklebank	
Tho: Park		Henry Fleminge	
Edw: Park		Willm Wilson	
Wm Wilson		Rodgr Atkinson	
Rowland Jackson		Row: Willson	
Wm Dilacre		John Willson	
James Park		Rich: Atkinson	
John Stillen		Isabell Dawson	
Edw: Park		James Willson	

Figure 3. *Manor of Torver, Lancashire, 1649 and 1664. Transcript of the names of copyhold tenants from a Parliamentary survey of 1649 and a later survey of 1664. Sequences of names in the top half of the 1649 list correlate with sequences in the bottom half of the 1664 list and vice versa. Most of the changes in tenancy can be traced in the court books.*

Other records

Apart from the court rolls, there are a number of other very informative manorial documents that should not be overlooked.

Verdicts are the draft minutes made at the time of the court by the clerk. They contain crossings out and alterations that do not appear in the final copy, sometimes of cases that were never heard. Plate XI shows a court baron verdict with a deleted comment at the bottom.[62] Plate XII is the certificate referred to in the deleted note. There may be other evidence, such as extracts from earlier courts, whose records may no longer exist.

Verdicts may be bound together with surrenders, the actual signed papers of an alienation of land to a new tenant. Surrenders are usually in English and may be annotated (as in Plate VIII). They may be accompanied by letters giving power of attorney to a friend or relation which in themselves often give details of relationships not mentioned in the surrender.

Mortgages were special surrenders that are often found among the records. Mortgage means literally 'dead pledge' (the land was passive security for a loan). Less common were live or living gages, where the land was handed over in exchange for a loan, with the lender taking the profits until the debt was paid off. Both sorts of gage should give detailed descriptions of the land in question, and sometimes information about its previous tenants.

Gages can provide information on the economic state of individuals. A series of mortgages for the Lancashire manor of Muchland in the eighteenth century show that William Geldart borrowed several sums of money against pieces of land over a number of months, at an interest rate of four shillings in five pounds (4%). The sums he borrowed were all fairly small, most were less than fifty pounds. Shortly after his last mortgage he lent out £400, the total of his borrowings, at 5%![63]

Mortgages may also provide information on the destination of emigrants who some-times lent or borrowed in their old community where they were better known.

A surrender to the use of a will (to the terms of a will) was a device, used before 1815, by which a tenant could bequeath copyhold land. The tenant making such a surrender would normally do so soon after being admitted to the property. Extracts from the parts of the will relating to the surrender may be found in the court baron record.

Surveys are descriptions of manors. They can be divided into three main types – terriers, extents and rentals.

Terriers are topographical accounts of manors giving the whereabouts of the demesne and tenements. They do not usually give details of individual tenants.

An Extent is a valuation of the manor and its tenancies, including land, buildings, rents, duties of the tenants and other incomes. It will normally include a list of the tenants.

During the period 1649-53 surveys (extents) were made of all Crown and Church lands before their sale by Parliament. These surveys provide descriptions of almost all Crown and ecclesiastical properties in England and Wales, including details of demesne land, annual income from rents, topographical information and the names of the tenants, both copyhold and freehold. The Parliamentary Survey of Crown Lands is now in The National Archives (Series E 317, with transcripts in DL 32 and LR 2). The Church surveys are more dispersed, being found in diocesan records, Lambeth Palace Library, the House of Lords Record Office and the British Library. After the Restoration, former Crown properties were returned to the Crown and again surveys were undertaken; they are also to be found in The National Archives (Series SC 11).

The first court baron held after the entry of a new lord was a court of recognition. Here he became seised of the services of the tenants who paid him a small fine often called 'certain knowledge'. Each tenant came before the lord, or the steward, with the copy of his admission or the deeds of his freeholding. After taking the oaths of fealty and homage the tenant was admitted as a tenant of the new lord. This was recorded along with the rent and services due from him, thus enabling the new lord to take stock of the manor and review the tenancies which were held of him.[64]

Rentals are lists of tenants showing the rents due from them at half-yearly intervals (normally Lady Day and Michaelmas). The lists were often drawn up yearly and include the tenant's name, the property and rent due. Some are annotated with the names of new tenants following a death or alienation.

Today we would consider a property survey without a map or plan to be incomplete, but maps were rare until the middle of the eighteenth century. However it may be possible to identify your ancestor's holding on tithe or enclosure maps.

Both rentals and extents give lists of tenants' names. In some lists the names are arranged alphabetically, in others they may appear to be random. In the latter case it is likely that there is a topographical arrangement, the list being by tenement rather than tenant. Try comparing lists a few years apart for a pattern of names (this may be easier if you have access to a computer with spread sheet software).

The appearance or disappearance of names in a sequence of annual rentals indicates that land has changed hands during the year. Details of the admission should appear in the court books within a couple of years; thus the rentals themselves can serve as an index to the books. Figure 3 shows the names of the tenants of Torver in 1649 and 1664.[65] The names are arranged by tenement rather than by tenant and most of the changes in name can be accounted for in the court book for the period.[66] The names of most of their properties can be identified from a chapelry rate assessment for 1671.[67]

The records of the manor were, of course, not created in total isolation. Alongside them, more general estate records were being generated, and valuable information can be gleaned from them. Among the records left by Sir Daniel Fleming of Rydal in Westmorland, is an account book or 'Book of Tenants',[68] in which he details thousands of transactions such as loans, sales of livestock, hides and other produce and payments for work carried out by local craftsmen. These accounts provide much insight into the financial dealings of his tenants; the price paid for cattle enables the size of herds to be calculated from probate inventories, which often give only a value; regular payments to a man for carrying out craft work may indicate that this was his main occupation, despite his being referred to as 'yeoman' or 'husbandman' in other records. The estate records of Viscount Lonsdale and Lord Clifford may well provide information about the tenants on their freeholdings at Beetham (*see* Plate I).

Printed transcripts have been made of a number of manorial records. They tend to be of medieval court rolls, but a few later ones do occur. They can usually be found in published Transactions of the various county antiquarian/archaeological societies or in local history societies' publications. A number (such as the court leet records for Manchester from 1552 to 1846) have been published privately.[69]

FINDING THE RECORDS

Manorial records may be in any of a number of places. It has already been shown that they may be in private hands. Many have been deposited in county record offices, some are in The National Archives and yet more are in the muniment rooms of various estates. A great many, particularly deeds, are to be found in solicitors' offices. The records of a single manor may be deposited in a number of repositories; those of the manor of Torver are to be found in county record offices of Cumbria and Lancashire, in The National Archives and in private hands. It is worth remembering that many large estates were spread across the country so that, for instance, the records of the Duke of Norfolk's manors in the north are kept in the muniment room at Arundel Castle.

The Law of Property (Amendment) Act of 1924 placed all manorial documents 'under the charge and superintendence' of the Master of the Rolls. Successive Masters have issued statutory rules for their custody: they must either remain in the hands of the lord of the manor (or his steward) or be deposited in an approved repository; they may not leave England or Wales without the permission of the Master of the Rolls – which has never been given; and they should be accessible for research, but do remember that they are private property. If they have been deposited they should be listed in a prescribed manner and a copy of the list forwarded to the Royal Commission on Historical Manuscripts for inclusion in the Manorial Documents Register, details of the Commission can be found in the Glossary.

The Manorial Documents Register is available for inspection. It consists of two parts, both arranged by county. The first part is on a slip index arranged by parish and lists all the known manors lying within the parish. The second part is arranged by manor within the county. This refers to lists of the documents that have been deposited, their location and the name and address of the last known lord of the manor and steward. However, in a number of cases the information is not up to date, nor is it truly comprehensive. The Manorial Documents Register for the whole of Wales and for Yorkshire and Hampshire, including the Isle of Wight, have been revised by the Historic Manuscripts Commission and converted to a computer database, which is accessable via the Internet at www.hmc.gov.uk. Work is now being carried out in association with Norfolk Record Office to make the Norfolk manors available on the Inernet and the Commission is investigating funding and stategies for computerising the rest of England. If you cannot find a reference in the register ask at the relevant county record office, where there will often be an index to its own holdings and the staff may have local knowledge as to the whereabouts of private collections.

The National Archives has a great number of manorial records of all types. Mention has been already been made of surveys held there, but there are also court rolls and books, particularly for the second half of the sixteenth century when the Crown was still holding former monastic lands (Series SC 2, SC 11, DL 30 and DL 43). The Crown held many manors until 1926 and records of a number of them are to be found among the Crown Estate papers at The National Archives (Series CRES 5).

Many Welsh manorial records are deposited with the National Library of Wales as Estate Papers.

The *Victoria County History* volumes give histories of many manors, with details of the successive lords since Domesday. This may help in locating records for a particular period. These manorial histories usually have copious footnotes, which provide additional information on secondary sources and transcripts. Lords of the manor were also noted in the various county trades directories, which may also record the names of manors of which each parish or township was a part.

APPENDIX

Transcript of presentments by manorial juries in 1725 and 1728, concerning the customs of land use, given as evidence in an objection to Enclosure in 1796.[70]

Mannor of Walton Thames

Nineteenth day of July One thousand seven hundred and twenty five, at a Court then held.

It is Presented (as follows Viz;) We Present an antient Custom belonging to the Tennants of the Mannor that after the death of a Copyholder his Widow to hold and enjoy the same during her life, altho' she marry again Paying her free Bench and after to descend to the younger Son or younger Daughter, which said Custom have been time out of Mind.

Item We present an antient Custom time out of Mind for the Tennants of this Mannor to cut Heath and Turf in any part of the waste of this Mannor Except the low Commons called Sharp Thornes laying below the way leading from the Town to the School House and reaching to Feild Common And we do Amerce them that shall cut any contrary to this our Order or that have cut any since the first day of May One thousand seven hundred and five the Sum of four shillings for every load so cut one half to the Lord of the Mannor and the other half to the Informer.

Item We Present an antient Custom time out of Mind for the Tennants of this Mannor to dig Sand Loam or Gravell upon any part of the Waste of this Mannor for necessary repairs without leave of the Lord of the said Mannor.

Item We present an antient Custom time out of mind for the Tennants of this Mannor to Fell Elm Ash or Withy from their Copyholds and to dispose of the same as they shall think fit, without the leave of the Lord of the said Mannor.

Item We present an antient Custom time out of Mind for the Tennants of this Mannor to Fell Oak Timber from their Copyhold for necessary Repairs upon his Copyhold Estate with out leave of the Lord of the Mannor.

Item We present an antient Stint of Commonage time out of mind for sheep (that is to say) three Sheep for an Acre and ten for a Messuage or Tenement and do amerce every person that Exceeds this Stint three Shillings and four pence for every score exceeding such Stint so often as they shall be taken so offending.

Item We do order that no Sheep shall be kept in any of the Common Feilds until fourteen days after the sowed feilds are cleared of Corn and do Amerce the Owners of any such Sheep one Shilling and Eight pence for every Score that shall be kept contrary to this our Order.

Item We do Order that no Sheep shall be kept of the Common Feilds after twenty Acres are sown in the said feild on pain of paying four pence for every Score so offending and proportionable for a greater or lesser Number.

Item We Order that no person shall keep or bait any Cattle or Hoggs in any of the said Common Feilds until the said Feilds are cleared of Corn on pain of paying four pence for every head of Cattle and twopence a head for hogs to the pounder for his pains for every default.

Item We do Order that every person that shall sell or deliver any Heath or Turf to any person being no Tennant of this Mannor or having no right to the same shall pay for every Load or Carriage of Heath or Turf so sold or delivered ten shillings one moiety to the Lord of the Mannor and the other to the Informer.

Item We present a Common Fine due to the Lord of this Mannor the Sum of two Shillings and six pence to be paid by the Headbourough.

Item Whereas it has been practised sometime past that the Tennants of a Mannor Court being then upon the Jury have given Leave by the Consent of the Lord to several persons to inclose ground of the Waste unknown to the rest of the Tennants of this Mannor to the prejudice of the major part who were not privy to the same We therefore Order that no person for the future shall inclose any ground of the Waste without the general Consent of all the said Tennants of the said Mannor every Tennant having an equal Right to the Herbage with those of the Homage.

Walton Thames. The fourteenth day of October one thousand seven hundred and twenty five, at a Court then held, tis presented as follows (viz')

We present that the Waste or Common has never been Severed.

Item We order that no person shall keep or bait any cattle or hoggs in the Common Feilds untill the feild be rid of Corn unless upon their own land or in Cottemore upon pain of paying four pence for every head of cattle and two pence a head for Hogs so found and taken by the pounder, who shall have the said money for his pains so often as they are taken.

Item We order that no horses or Cows shall be kept or pastured upon the Waste Ground in the Common feilds Except Cottemore only untill the said feilds be cleared of Corn and do Amerce the Owners so taken one shilling for every Horse or Cow, all the other presentments of this Court are to the same effect as at the former Court held the nineteenth day of July one thousand seven hundred and twenty five Except the presentment of a common fine of two shillings and sixpence to the Lord to be paid by the Headborough, which is not presented here.

Walton Thames. Tenth October one thousand seven hundred and twenty eight, at the Court held, tis presented as follows

Item We present an antient Custom time out of mind for the Tennants of this Manner to cut heather and Turfe in any part of the Waste of this Manner Except in the low Common called Sharp Thorns lying below the way leading from the Towne to the School house and reaching to Field Common and we do amerce them that shall cut any contray to this our Order after the seventh day of May one thousand six hundred and ninety nine five shillings for every load so carried to be levied on them that shall cut or carry the same one part to the Informer and the other part to the Lord of the Mannor.

All the other presentments at this Court to be the same Effect as before.

NOTES AND REFERENCES

1 I am indebted to Mrs Mari Alderman for this information.
2 Travers, *Manorial Documents.*
3 Kerridge, *Agrarian problems*, p.1.
4 Kerridge, *Agrarian problems*, p.18.
5 Encyclopedia Britannica: *Feudalism.*
6 Beaumont, W, 'Homage Roll of the Manor of Warrington', in *Miscellanies: Lancashire and Cheshire vol.I.* Lancashire and Cheshire Record Society 12, 1885.
7 Steward's Notebook of six Surrey manors. Surrey Record Office: 174/4/1.
8 Simpson, A W B, *An Introduction to the History of Land Law.* Oxford University Press, (1961), p.162.
9 Gloucestershire Record Office: D2240 Box 1. I am indebted to Paul Blake for drawing my attention to this document.
10 Stephens, *Sources,* p.74.
11 Marshall, J D, *Furness and the industrial revolution,* Barrow-in-Furness Public Library Committee, 1958, p.129.
12 Baker, *English legal history*, p.27.
13 Kerridge, *Agrarian problems*, p.54.
14 Simpson, A W B, *An Introduction to the History of Land Law.* Oxford University Press, (1961), p .56.
15 Simpson, A W B, *An Introduction to the History of Land Law.* Oxford University Press, (1961), pp .67 and 90.
16 Baker, *English legal history,* p.218; Statute of Wills (32 Hen VIII, c1).
17 Kerridge, *Agrarian problems,* p.88.
18 Kerridge, *Agrarian problems,* p.60.
19 Kerridge, *Agrarian problems,* p.48.
20 Cumbria Archives, Kendal: WD/AG/1.
21 Kerridge, p.50; Macfarlane, A, *Reconstructing historical communities,* Cambridge University Press, 1977, p.49.
22 Baker, *English legal history,* pp.126-8.
23 Baker, *English legal history,* p.224.
24 Kerridge, *Agrarian problems,* p.37.
25 Simpson, A W B, *An Introduction to the History of Land Law.* Oxford University Press, (1961), pp.51-52.
26 Simpson, A W B, *An Introduction to the History of Land Law.* Oxford University Press, (1961), p.21.
27 Baker, *English legal history,* p.225-6.
28 Kerridge, *Agrarian problems,* p.54.
29 Sir Daniel Fleming's Book of tenants (late seventeenth century), Cumbria Archives, Kendal: WD/Ry/21.
30 Cumbria Archives, Barrow: BD/HJ/200/10.
31 Cumbria Archives, Barrow: BD/HJ/200/12.
32 Travers
33 Riden, P, *Record sources for local history,* 1987, p.43.

34 The use of Latin and Court Hand was repealed in 1731 (4 Geo. II c26); The Manchester court leet rolls were in English from as early as 1552, see also note 69.
35 Cumbria Archives, Kendal: WD/AG/1.
36 Kerridge, *Agrarian problems,* p.67.
37 Cumbria Archives, Barrow: BD/HJ/194/14/1
38 Lancashire Record Office: DDHj, Torver court book, 1740-53.
39 'Queen's councell' – the Queen was the Lady of this manor.
40 Cumbria Archives, Barrow: BD/HJ/200/13.
41 Webb, S and B, 'The manor and the borough Part I', p.4 et seq, 1926. *English local government vol.2.*
42 Cumbria Archives, Barrow: BD/HJ/200/13.
43 Webb p.70.
44 Torver court book, 1740-53, Lancashire Record Office: DDHj.
45 Cumbria Archives, Barrow: BD/HJ/200/10.
46 Torver court book, 1740-53. Lancashire Record Office: DDHj.
47 Lancashire Record Office: DDX/474.
48 Cumbria Archives, Barrow: BD/HJ/198.
49 Cumbria Archives, Barrow: BD/HJ/191.
50 Baker p.210-211.
51 10 Edw. VII c.8.
52 Cumbria Archives, Barrow: BD/HJ/200/11.
53 Cumbria Archives, Barrow: BD/HJ/200/11.
54 Cumbria Archives, Barrow: BD/HJ/200/10.
55 Cumbria Archives, Barrow: BD/HJ/200/10.
56 Cumbria Archives, Barrow: BD/HJ/200/10.
57 Cumbria Archives, Barrow: BD/HJ/200/10. A 'hubleshow' was approximately disturbing the peace
58 Cumbria Archives, Barrow: BD/HJ/200/9.
59 Cumbria Archives, Barrow: BD/HJ/200/10.
60 Park, P B, 'A turbulent priest' in Cumbria FHS *Newsletter,* No.53 (November 1989), pp.3-5.
61 Cumbria Archives, Barrow: BD/HJ/200/10.
62 Cumbria Archives, Barrow: BD/HJ/200/13.
63 Public Record Office: CRES/5.
64 Kerridge, *Agrarian problems,* p.25.
65 Parliamentary survey of the manor of Muchland including the bailiwicks of Torver and Newbiggin, 1649, PRO: E 317/Lancashire 18; and Copyhold rental of the manor of Torver, 1664, PRO: SC 2/916.
66 Cumbria Archives, Barrow: BD/HJ/200/13 & 14.
67 Brierley, H. 'The registers of the parish church of Torver', *Lancashire Parish Register Society,* 43, 1911, pages 91-2.
68 Fleming, see note 30.
69 *Manchester Court Leet,* published in twelve volumes by the City of Manchester in 1884. It is of note that, from the earliest volume, the records of the courts were in English. Copy in the Library of the Society of Genealogists.
70 Surrey RO: 97/2/17i.

BIBLIOGRAPHY

Most county antiquarian/historical societies publish articles on various aspects of local manors in their Transactions. The *Victoria County History* series has a great deal of information on the manors in each of the counties covered, particularly giving details about successive lords.

Alcock, N W. *Old title deeds*, Phillimore, 1986.

Baker. J H, *An Introduction to English Legal History*, Butterworths, (1979).

Colwell, Stella, *The Family History Book,* Phaidon, (1989). Pages 102-106 deal with land ownership, including manorial tenures.

Dibben, A A. *Title Deeds*, Historical Association, Help for students of history series, No.72, (1990)

Encyclopedia Britannica (1970) The following entries are particularly useful: Manor; Feudal System; English Law; Court Baron; Court Leet; Real Property and Conveyancing.

Gooder, Eileen A, *Latin for Local History,* Longman, (1978). As well as the grammar it has useful lists of words and common abbreviations.

Harvey, P D A, *Manorial Records,* British Record Association, Archives and the User Series No.5. (1984) Probably the most authoritative and readable general introduction to manorial records and to the system that generated them.

Jessel, C. *The law of the manor*, Barry Rose Law Publishers, (1998)

Kerridge, Eric, *Agrarian Problems in the Sixteenth Century and After,* George Allen and Unwin, (1969) A good introduction to the legal complexities of manorial tenure.

Morris, Jane, *A Latin Glossary for Family and Local Historians,* FFHS, (1989). Very useful list of words and common abbreviations – more extensive than Gooder.

Palgrave-Moore, Patrick, *How to Locate and Use Manorial Records,* Elvery Dowers, (1985).

Richardson, John, *The Local Historian's Encyclopedia,* Historical Publications, (1986). Particularly good for explanations of many obscure terms used to describe tenures, inheritance, etc.

Riden, Philip, *Record Sources for Local History*, Batsford, (1986).

Simpson, A W B, *An Introduction to the History of Land Law*. Clarendon Press, (1986).

Stuart, D. *Manorial records*, Phillimore, (1992). Discusses interpretation and palaeography of manorial records, mainly for an earlier period than this booklet.

Thompson, E P, 'The Grid of Inheritance', in Goody, Thirsk and Thompson. *Family and Inheritance: Rural Society in Western Europe 1200-1800,* Cambridge UP, (1978). Discusses inheritance with particular reference to manorial customs.

Travers, Anita, 'Manorial Documents', *Genealogists Magazine,* 21 (1) 1-9. A useful short introduction with examples of genealogical use of the records.

Webb, S and B, *'The manor and the borough Part I',* (1926). English local government vol.2: *The manor and the borough, Part I,* reprint by Frank Cass, (1963). Gives copious examples of documents, mainly transcribed, for the period after 1685.

GLOSSARY

Note: Many of these words have precise legal meanings, but were often used more loosely by court clerks. There may also be some minor differences in meaning between geographical regions.

admission The acceptance of a new tenant into a tenement. The record of the acceptance in the manor court rolls. *See also* alienation and surrender.

affeeror Official appointed to assess penalties for offences. Often called assessor.

ale taster An official of the court leet who checked the quality and measurement of ale (and sometimes bread) for sale on the manor. Also known as ale conner or ale founder.

alienation Transfer of a customary tenancy. After agreement between the vendor and buyer (usually a deed was drawn up) the tenement was surrendered to the lord before the incoming tenant was admitted on payment of his fine at the next court baron. Between surrender and admission, the buyer had use of the property, but could not alienate it. *See also* admission, surrender and use.

amercement Money penalty paid in court; note that the word fine *(qv)* had a specific meaning.

appurtenance Right associated with a tenancy, for instance, grazing a specified number of cattle on the waste, or cutting turves.

arbitrary fine Fine *(qv)* the value of which was negotiated (arbitrated) between the incoming tenant and the lord. The affeerors would assess the fine to ensure that it was reasonable. *See also* fine certain.

assart Woodland which had been cleared, enclosed and converted into arable land. Sometimes spelled essert.

assessor *See* affeeror.

attachment *See* distraint.

attorney Legal representative; letters giving power of attorney are sometimes to be found with surrenders.

bailiff The lord's representative on the manor. Often a tenant himself. Sometimes called greave or reeve.

barleyman Official of the court baron responsible for enforcement of its customary or bye-law orders. Also called bylawman, burleyman or paynelooker.

baron, court Manorial court where the lord enforced his rights to rents and services and where the tenants rights were protected by the customs of the manor. Without the right to hold this court there was no manor, just an 'estate'. It could also fulfil a local, judicial role. *See also* leet, court.

barony A number of manors held directly of the Crown by the same lord (tenant-in-chief), often having its own courts. May be subdivided into smaller groups or lordships *(qv)*.

bartonland *See* bordland.

benefit *See* use.

Border tenant-right Military service, common in Cumberland, Westmorland, North Lancashire, North Yorkshire, Northumberland and Durham. It provided customary tenants with low, fixed rents, but on condition that they provided armed men for a given number of days a year for service against the Scots as required. After the accession of James I in 1604, it was largely discontinued, but it was the basis for a number of disputes in the courts over the next hundred years or so.

bordland Copyhold tenure of demesne land at the will of the lord, but not according to the custom of the manor. Sometimes called new copyhold, netehold, roveless or runningland. *See also* demise.

Borough English Inheritance by youngest son (or daughter), found mainly in East Anglia. Sometimes called cradle hold. *See also* heir.

bote The right of tenants to take wood from the common, normally for a specific use, hence: Cartbote – to make or mend carts; firebote – for fuel; fencebote (or haybote) – for fences; housebote – for houses; ploughbote – for ploughs. *See also* estover.

burleyman See barleyman.

burrage Form of free tenure in ancient boroughs with certain rent.

bylawman See barleyman.

call book Register of those who owed suit to the court. Absentees were liable to amercement. *See also* essoin and defaulter.

cartbote *See* bote.

certain knowledge Fine paid to a new lord.

constable *See* petty constable.

copyhold tenure Usually a customary tenure, where the tenant was protected by title written in the manor court rolls of which he retained a copy – hence copyhold. Originally it carried an obligation to perform services, but these services were later commuted to cash payments called quit rents *(qv)*. Copyhold tenancies were finally abolished in 1926. *See also* bordland, customary tenure and tenant by the verge.

courtdeal *See* bordland.

court of recognition The first court held after the entry of a new lord, where he became seised of the services of the tenants.

court rolls/books Minutes of the courts. Early minutes were written on parchment membranes which were stitched together to form long strips which were rolled up for storage. By Tudor times the minutes were increasingly bound in book form.

cradle hold *See* Borough English.

customary tenure The majority of tenures were held at the will of the lord according to the customs of the manor and referred to as customary. Most, but not all, customary tenants in the early modern period had copies of entries in the manor court rolls recording their holdings, they were thus commonly called copyholders. *See also* tenant by the verge and copyhold tenure.

custumal Written details of the customs of the manor, including services due from tenants and the obligations of the lord. Often recorded when there was a change of lord.

dale *See* dole.

defaulter Tenant who fails to attend a court without good reason; liable to be amerced. *See also* essoin.

demesne Part of the manor reserved for the use of the lord. Might be rented out at the will of the lord. *See also* demise and bordland.

demise Tenancy by lease of demesne land *(qv)*; not subject to manorial custom. *See also* bordland.

disseisin Dispossession of an estate. *See also* seisin.

distraint Seizure of chattels of a person until he or she obeys an order laid down by the court. Often referred to as an attachment.

dole Portion of common meadow allocated to a tenant. Also called a dale or lot meadow.

doom Judgement of the court.

doorkeeper A minor official who checked that only those who were entitled to attended the court.

dower *See* freebench.

entail *See* fee tail.

escheat Reversion of land held in fee simple to the lord. Typically when a tenant died without an heir, had committed an offence (normally a felony) which incurred forfeiture of his estate, or sometimes where the heir was a minor.

essert *See* assart.

essoin Excuse for non-attendance at the manor court. A suitor was commonly allowed up to three consecutive essoins before amercement.

estover Necessaries allowed by law, especially wood for repairs allowed to a tenant from the lord's or a neighbour's estate, but also included such things as free-bench *(qv)* and maintenance for an imprisoned felon. *See also* bote.

extent Summary valuation of the manor and tenancies, including land, buildings, services and other income. *See also* survey.

fealty Oath of allegiance to the Crown made by incoming tenant. *See also* homage, 1).

fee An estate of inheritance – an interest in the land which will not necessarily come to an end on the death of an individual tenant, but is capable of being inherited. *See also* fee simple and fee tail.

fee simple An estate of inheritance where the heir was ascertained by applying the canons of descent. When there was no heir then the land passed to the feudal lord by escheat *(qv)*.

fee tail Similar to fee simple, but the heir must have been a descendant of the original tenant and not a collateral or ancestor.

feudal system Landholding system whereby land was held by a vassal of a superior lord (ultimately the King) in return for services, homage, etc. Largely abolished by statute in 1660.

fief A method of income devolved from a higher level in the feudal system. Normally land, but may also be the right to mill corn, etc.

fine Money payment to the lord made by an incoming tenant. *See also* arbitrary fine, fine certain and relief.

fine certain Fine *(qv)* fixed by the customs of the manor. *See also* arbitrary fine.

firebote *See* bote.

firehouse *See* messuage.

frankpledge A Saxon system, whereby a group, originally of about ten householders (a tithing), were collectively held responsible for the behaviour of individual members. *See also* view of frankpledge.

frank tenure Land tenure governed by common law – usually freehold.

freebench The custom that allowed a widow to become the tenant of the whole or part of her late husband's customary estate for life, or in some manors until she remarried. Usually with the proviso that she remained chaste. Sometimes called widows bench, widows estate or dower, although the latter term may denote freehold property.

freehold Tenure not subject to customs of the manor, but governed by common law. *See also* fee.

gavelkind Division of a holding between all the sons on the death of the tenant. Although abolished by Henry VII, it survived in some areas – notably in Kent – until 1926. *See also* partible inheritance.

greave *See* bailiff.

gressom A fine *(qv)*.

halmote A manorial court.

haybote *See* bote.

hayward Official of the court baron whose duty was to check that fences etc. were in good repair.

headborough *See* petty constable.

hedgelooker *See* hayward.

heir Person entitled to inherit property etc. See also Borough English, primogeniture and partible inheritance.

heriot Payment in kind to the lord on the death of a tenant; traditionally the 'best beast'. Sometimes commuted to a cash payment.

homage, (1) Oral acknowledgement by a tenant of his loyalty and feudal obligations to his lord. See also fealty.

homage (2) Assembly of tenants acting as a jury at a court baron.

housebote *See* bote.

houselooker Minor official of the court baron, who checked that houses and other buildings were kept habitable.

impartible Estate or tenement which cannot be divided.

incidents Various incomes of the lord from the manor, such as fines, amercements and heriots.

jury Assembly of tenants in a court sworn to reach a verdict *(qv)* on the matter submitted. Sometimes called the homage.

knight service Military service due under a freehold tenure. It was abolished in 1660, by which time it had usually been commuted to a cash payment. *See also* Border tenant right.

leet, court A manorial court. A minor Crown court where petty offences were tried. Not all manors had a leet jurisdiction. See also baron, court and view of frankpledge.

lives *See* tenancy for lives.

livery of seisin Procedure for the transfer of possession of tenancy or ownership.

living gage Conditional surrender where the lender has the use of the land until it pays off the loan. *See also* mortgage and use.

lord of the manor Landlord, holding a manor directly from the Crown or via a lord or tenant-in-chief.

lordship Small group of manors with the same lord, who held them of a tenant-in-chief, rather than directly of the Crown. *See also* barony.

lot meadow *See* dole.

manor An estate held by a lord and having a court baron *(qv)* jurisdiction. *See also* lord of the manor.

manor court *See* baron and leet.

Manorial Documents Register The Law of Property (Amendment) Act of 1924 placed all manorial documents 'under the charge and superintendence' of the Master of the Rolls. Under his authority the Manorial Documents Register was compiled. Since 1958 it has been maintained at the offices of the Royal Commission on

Historical Manuscripts *(qv)*, where it is available for public inspection. It consists of two parts, both arranged by county. The first is a slip index arranged by parish and lists all known manors within a parish. The second, arranged by manor, consists of lists of manorial documents supplied by lords, stewards or record repositories. Part of the manorial Documents Register for Yorkshire, Wales and Hampshire, including the Isle of Wight is available on the Internet at: http://www.hmc.gov.uk ***Note that the Royal Commission on Historical Manuscripts holds no documents itself, but only records their whereabouts.***

mesne lord Lord holding land directly from the Crown.

messuage A dwelling house.

moot A meeting.

mortgage A conveyance of land as security against a debt. For customary property the mortgage took the form of a conditional surrender – the property was surrendered to the lord until such time as the debt was paid when the surrender became void. The debtor retained the use of the property. *See also* living gage, surrender and use.

new copyhold *See* bordland.

netehold *See* bordland.

pain Penalty or punishment, in customary law often prescribed for a specific offence. Upon or under pain – threat of penalty for not fulfilling an order or condition of a court. Against pain – penalty for defiance of a previous order of the court.

pannage Tenant's right to feed hogs in the common woods.

parcener One who shares, a partner.

partible inheritance System allowing a tenement or estate to be divided on the death of the tenant, or by sale. *See also* gavelkind.

payne looker *See* barleyman.

petty constable Officer responsible for local law and order. Under the feudal system he was usually appointed by the court leet, but sometimes by the court baron; later the appointment was made by the vestry. He was sometimes called headborough or tithingman. Often referred to, incorrectly, as 'parish constable'.

pinder A minor manor official who rounded up stray animals; their owners were liable to amercement.

ploughbote *See* bote.

presentment Report of the homage on a matter brought for its consideration. Most commonly alienation in the court baron, but a range of minor offences at the court leet.

primogeniture Inheritance by eldest son. *See also* heir.

quit rent Annual payment to the lord in lieu of services due.

reeve *See* bailiff.

relief Payment made by an heir to succeed to a freehold inheritance; often the value of the annual rent. *See also* fine.

rental List of tenants with details of rents due and paid. *See also* survey.

reversion Return of land to the donor or grantor or his heir where there are no heirs to a fee tail *(qv)* at the end of a life tenancy or at the end of a lease. The donor was not necessarily the lord of the manor, he may have been a freeholder.

rod *See* tenant by the verge.

roveless *See* bordland.

Royal Commission on Historical Manuscripts Quality House, Quality Court, Chancery Lane, London, WC2A 1HP. Telephone 020 7242 1198. Internet site: http://www.hmc.gov.uk

runningland *See* bordland.

seisin Possession of property; strictly freehold, but often used referring to customary holdings. *See also* disseisin.

seised Having legal possession.

socage A form of freehold tenure, without the obligation of military service.

staff *See* tenant by the verge.

steward Agent of the lord. He was usually a lawyer; the position of deputy steward was one of the recognised means of livelihood for young lawyers at the beginning of the seventeenth century.

straw *See* tenant by the verge.

suit of court Attendance required of tenants, or others, by a manor court.

surrender The first part in the alienation of a customary tenure, when the land was handed back to the lord in trust for the new tenant before he was admitted at the next court baron. The document recording such a transfer. *See also* admission, alienation and mortgage.

survey An account of a manor, usually one of three types: extents, rentals or terriers *(qv)*.

tenancy-at-will Tenure granted by the lord with terms and conditions at his discretion, although by common law they had to be 'reasonable'.

tenancy for lives Prevalent in some parts of the country especially the west of England and also on Church and college manors, typically for three lives. They were copyhold and usually subject to arbitrary fines (those not regulated by manorial custom). A life could be added, at the lord's discretion, on the death of the tenant or his successors.

tenant Legal occupier of a parcel of land on the manor, paying rent and/or services to the lord.

tenant by the verge A customary tenant who did not hold by copy, but otherwise the same as a copyholder. The tenant was given seisin by the acceptance of a verge (a ceremonial rod or staff), a straw or symbolic clod of earth. See also customary tenure. Sometimes 'admitted by the rod' in the court rolls.

tenant-in-chief Tenant holding land directly from the Crown.

tenement A parcel of land occupied by a tenant. See also customary tenure, copyhold tenure, freehold, tenancy for lives and tenancy-at-will.

terrier Topographical account of the manor, giving whereabouts and size of the lord's and the tenants' land. *See also* survey.

time out of mind/time immemorial Beyond legal memory, in theory before 1189, but in practice not always so.

tithing A group, originally, of ten men or households. *See also* frankpledge.

turbary Common right to dig peat or turf for fuel on the waste or common.

use Benefit or profit of tenement in the hands of the lord, who holds them for the beneficiary. *See also* alienation and mortgage.

vassal Tenant who owed services and homage to a lord.

verdict Decision of the jury or homage or the document recording the decision.

view of frankpledge Twice a year the headman of each tithing *(qv)* attended the hundred court to report on the state of law and order in his locality – this was the view of frankpledge. It was from this that the manorial court leet developed. *See also* frankpledge and leet, court.

widow's bench or estate *See* freebench.

will of the lord Conditions of tenure not subject to the customs of the manor, but at the discretion of the lord.

INDEX

Note: This index does not include entries in the Glossary.

The Parish Ch
ST LEON
HYTHE, KENT

Hythe means 'haven'; it was one of the original Cinque Ports required to provide ships and men for England's defence in return for tax relief and other privileges. In the years of prosperity that followed William the Conqueror's invasion of 1066 – a great period of ecclesiastical building – the citizens of Hythe built a magnificent new church in both the Norman and Early English styles. It was well-sited, standing on an important Continental trade and pilgrim route.

THREE CHURCHES IN ONE

Although it is now difficult to imagine, Hythe's rise and development stems from its former role as a busy Channel port. St Leonard's stands far from the sea today, but when the first Norman church was built, in *c.*1080, the High Street formed the quayside of the Cinque Port of Hythe.

The church is not mentioned in Domesday Book, but does appear in the Domesday Monachorum (that lists the ecclesiastical estates of the Archbishop of Canterbury), as Hethe Chapel and subject to the Manor of Saltwood. The church grew in size and importance as Hythe prospered, and it became a separate parish in 1844. Some experts believe that the north transept (now called St Edmund's Chapel or the Soldiers' Chapel) was once the site of Hythe's previous church: a Saxon-style arch and the curious conical tower alongside might be evidence of this.

Successive archbishops at Saltwood Castle are believed to have been responsible for its enlargement in c.1120 and c.1220, probably using cathedral masons and craftsmen.

RIGHT: St Leonard's window in the south porch. St Leonard, a hermit monk, founded a monastery near Limoges in the 6th century, and to his intercession were attributed many miracles. Returning crusaders looked upon him as the patron saint of prisoners. (1)

BELOW: A Mass dial from before the south porch was built, used to show when Mass would be celebrated. (2)

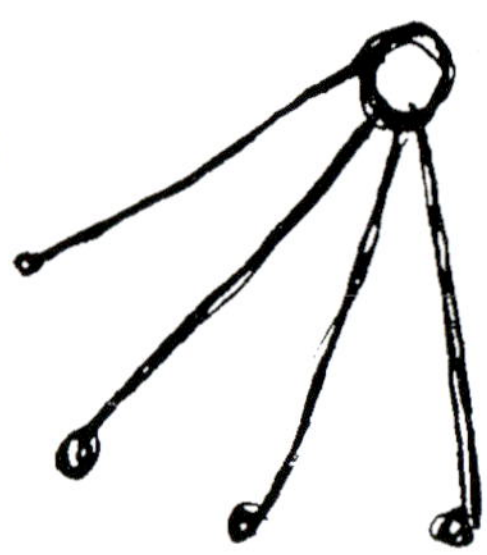

LEFT: A medieval gargoyle on the west tower c.1480.

Aisles and transepts were added and a new, more elaborate choir with a small apse was fashioned. Entry was through a west door where the interior tower wall now stands. Many Norman features can still be seen: the arches in the south aisle and in the choir vestry, as well as the remains of two windows above the north aisle.

By c.1220 pilgrims were arriving in Hythe on their way to Canterbury, visiting the church and St Leonard's relic. With their offerings the town made further enlargements, adding a magnificent three-storey chancel, side-chapels and screen in the Early English Gothic style. Beneath the impressive raised sanctuary was an ambulatory, probably designed for the relic to be borne in procession around the building without leaving consecrated ground.

The prosperity did not last: as the money ran out the westward nave arches become progressively smaller, and the chancel vaulting, the north triforium and the top windows were left unfinished until the 19th century. The 14th century saw the addition of a west tower, and a new south door with porch and room (parvise) above for the priest. The window for him to see into his church is still in place.

RIGHT: Before the choir vestry was built this superb Norman archway was an entrance to the church. When no longer needed it was bricked up and re-opened only in the 1860s. High up on the left-hand side is a human face with its tongue out in an unexplained derogatory gesture.

A TREASURE HOUSE OF DEVOTION

A worshipper in the Middle Ages would have entered a church full of wall paintings with vibrant reds, blues and greens – probably a lurid sight to the modern eye. Traces of this ancient paintwork can still be seen in the south aisle. The high chancel with its 13 steps was designed to allow for the growing trend towards processions during services. An ambulatory, or ceremonial passageway, was built underneath the altar so that the priest and his flock could process on holy ground around the church. The round tower, entered by a door near the pulpit, allowed access to the rood loft which topped a huge, overpowering carved wooden screen (demolished at the Reformation), dividing nave from chancel. Evidence of medieval devotion can be seen in the carved Easter sepulchre of the north transept and in the fine double piscina and sedilia by the high altar.

BELOW: *Over the steps at the south porch, in a room known as the parvise, was the old town hall used by the mayor and burgesses of Hythe until the late 18th century.*

On departure, pilgrims would often carve in the stonework a cross or other suitable emblem as an anticipatory thank offering to God for their safe journey. Many of these marks can still be seen clearly. Pilgrims came to St Leonard's in its own right, to pray and give donations for its upkeep. A cross in the centre of the rood screen is known to have had holy relics contained within. These caused a dispute between the rector and parishioners who according to their own wishes 'spent the offerings lavishly'. In 1252 Pope Innocent IV upbraided the parishioners for their actions.

In 1400 Pope Boniface IX directed that four priests should hear the confessions of pilgrims visiting the church. Those who gave money would also benefit from a spiritual indulgence which would allow them, it was thought, to enter heaven more easily.

ABOVE: *Carved onto the St Christopher pillar are pilgrim crosses and drawings of medieval ships. These are rare and date from the 13th century. They were probably carved by pilgrims in thanks for their safe arrival, presumably with the parish priest's consent!* (4)

Although the townsfolk were able to rebuild the chancel and the two transepts in the 13th century, after they had added the present tower and porch, money began to run out. Loss of life through plague, fire and storms came first. Then the sea retreated and during the 16th century the port entirely silted up.

Poignant evidence of the town's decline can be seen in the nave. Only one arch, near the north transept, has been rebuilt in the same style as the chancel. The nave arches become smaller and smaller towards the west tower. Even the chancel vaulting and the upper parts of the clerestory remained unfinished until the late 19th century.

'This is the finest chancel of any church in England, not to say Europe!'
PROFESSOR FRANCIS BOND
A RENOWNED AUTHORITY ON MEDIEVAL CHURCH ARCHITECTURE

THE CRYPT, A HOUSE OF BONES

Underneath the chancel is an area that was used for processions in the Middle Ages, and which now contains the largest and best-preserved collection of human skulls and bones in the United Kingdom. When and why the human remains were moved here is not known. The first recorded references to the house of bones and skulls were in 1678–79, whilst a drawing dated 1787 shows a collection of bones and skulls at the south main door. Past historians have argued that the collection was brought here in the 13th century when the chancel was extended into the former churchyard area, or during the 15th century, but these dates cannot be verified.

It was thought that the crypt contains the remains of 4,000 people, but from recent analysis the more likely estimate is 1,500-2,000. It has been argued that the remains were of Saxons or Danes killed in battle, but a 2010 study has identified that over half the skulls are female, whilst ten per cent are juveniles. This points to later theories that the remains were from the general population. As the graveyards of St Leonard's and other nearby churches had become full by the late Middle Ages, the remains were dug up and placed in the crypt so that the burial grounds could be reused.

Research studies during 2009–10 show that some of the skulls had suffered pre-death blows due to violence or accident. There is evidence of broken bones and distorted limbs due to arthritis, all of which would have been extremely painful. Pin-prick holes around numerous eye sockets show a high incidence of anaemia, possibly resulting from lack of iron in diet. However, most teeth are in good condition (in the absence of sugar!) although worn down by eating coarse bread.

LEFT: A skull showing damage caused by a heavy blow, due to violence or accident. (22)

'England's most celebrated ... ossuary'

SIMON JENKINS, 1999
ENGLAND'S THOUSAND BEST CHURCHES

LEFT: *A jawbone clearly showing teeth in remarkably good condition.* (22)

A CHURCH EVOLVING

During the Reformation the rich decoration that filled the church was stripped away. Wall paintings, rood screen and statues were destroyed, altars removed and pews added for the first time. Throughout the 16th and 17th centuries the interior would have appeared remarkably plain.

The west tower of the medieval church collapsed in 1739; possibly it had finally succumbed to weakness created by a severe earthquake of 1580. The ferocity of the tremors was reported to have made the church bells ring and caused dangerous cracks in nearby Saltwood Castle.

A newspaper reported: 'We learn from Hythe that on Thursday morning last, about eleven o'clock, the steeple of their church fell down, and that they have been busy digging out the bells, being six in number. About ten persons were present when it fell, waiting for the keys in the church porch to go up the steeple for a view. But some delay being made in bringing them, they all happily saved their lives, and had no other damage than being terribly frightened.'

BELOW: An aquatint (1823) by William Daniell before the renovation of the roof of the nave and transept. In the distance are a windmill and a line of Martello towers built c.1805 as part of the coastal defences against Napoleon.

RIGHT: The 'Armada' chest, a strongbox in which were kept registers and later parish moneys: hence three people, each with a key, had to be present to open it! (19)

The tower was subsequently reconstructed in 1750, using the old materials. The south transept was rebuilt the following year, largely through the generosity of the Deedes family, many of whose ancestors are buried there. There was a clock in the tower before 1413, although the present instrument dates from 1901. A peal of at least five bells is recorded before the 1480s. Subsequently there were normally eight, two bells being added in 1993 to make the full peal of ten.

In the 18th century there were galleries for the town's growing population; poorer people, servants and 'charity children' sat above, while the pews below were rented to wealthier worshippers. The St Edmund Chapel was for the soldiers of the School of Musketry established in 1853. The bricked-up doorway on the west wall was probably opened for their use – it was considered important to keep the classes separate. The mayor and corporation had designated pews; to this day councillors sit in the 'poppy-head pews'.

ABOVE: *Known today as the Calvary Chapel; before the Reformation this was the Lady Chapel.* ⑯

LIONEL LUKIN

The churchyard contains the grave of Lionel Lukin who patented the world's first lifeboat in 1785. Originally an Essex coachbuilder, he moved to Hythe in his retirement. His grave lies just to the west of the tower.

A TREASURE HOUSE RESTORED

ABOVE: The former reredos to the high altar is perhaps the finest treasure in the church. It was designed by George Street and sculpted by Henry Armstead. (17)

In 1875 and 1887 restorations to the church were carried out at a cost of £10,000. Two of the finest Victorian architects, George Street and John Pearson, were employed (Street designed the Law Courts in the Strand, Pearson the new cathedral for Truro). At St Leonard's the two men successfully completed many of the features which the original medieval craftsmen had intended to incorporate before the funds dried up. The vaulting to the chancel and aisle roofs was completed in 1887, albeit five centuries overdue. The present barrel-shaped roof in the nave dates from 1875. The pulpit, with its fine Venetian mosaic work, composed of 20,000 pieces, is of the same date.

Many of the fittings introduced at that time were in keeping with the medieval devotional life of the church. Amongst these is an especially fine marble reredos which originally stood behind the high altar, but is now situated in the south choir aisle. This is a masterpiece of artistic work, given by a former curate in memory of his wife. There is a Pre-Raphaelite touch in the depiction of the angels, and its deep swirling lines give it an almost sultry appearance. It was carved from a single piece of Carrara marble in 1881 by Henry Armstead to the designs of George Street. It was moved to its present position in 1938.

LEFT: The console of the fine Harrison organ.

Two features in the church bring the visitor abruptly into the 20th century. In the south aisle a remarkable stained-glass window commemorates 2nd Lieutenant Robert Hildyard who was killed, with over a million others, on the Somme in 1916. The window has a dreamy, surreal effect, and is a fine example of the art nouveau style. The present fine organ, built in 1936 by Harrison & Harrison, is the latest in a long line dating back to the 15th century.

ABOVE: *The pulpit replaced an 18th-century model which towered to twice the size: this was in order that those in the gallery could hear and see the delivery of the sermon.* ⑫

LEFT: *The Hildyard window, a poignant tribute to a young soldier killed in the First World War.* ⑥

ST LEONARD'S TODAY

ABOVE: The magnificent organ pipes at the west end of the nave.

Most visitors are impressed by the main east window which shows Christ, surrounded by angels, ascending to Heaven. The Victorian glass which once occupied the space was destroyed in 1940, when a German bomb struck the ground at the east end of the church, causing extensive damage. The present east window was dedicated in 1951 and reflects the long-term role played by the town of Hythe in the front line of England's defence. A Cinque Port ship can be seen in the panel at the bottom left, and an anti-aircraft gun and searchlights in the right-hand panel.

The only structural alteration to the church in the 20th century was the building of the choir vestry on the north side in 1959, enclosing the fine Norman arch added to the first church.

Worship at St Leonard's is enriched by its adult and junior choirs who sing in a variety of styles, including traditional forms of service. Its musical heritage is also maintained through concerts and recitals organised by the Friends of St Leonard's Church, held regularly in the church. Moreover, the church building is continually being developed and restored through the fundraising efforts of its parishioners.

St Leonard's remains passionately committed to exploring the mystery of God (also identified as 'the divine' or 'the sacred'), wherever it might be encountered: in the words of scripture, in the sacraments, in sacred music, in the beauty of this place and in the love shared between fellow searchers.

The dignified forms of service, coupled with the best of English church music, combine to deepen the spiritual health of all those who keep returning to seek God in a very special and holy place.